The
CREATIVE WRITING
Workbook

Matthew Branton

About the author

Matthew Branton is the author of the acclaimed novels *The House of Whacks, The Love Parade, Coast and The Hired Gun* (all for Bloomsbury) as well of *Write a Bestselling Thriller* (Hodder & Stoughton, 2012). He has also worked in fiction publishing, screenwriting, as a freelance journalist, and as a consultant for the Literary Consultancy of London. He enjoys surfing, hiking and gardening, and lives in Cornwall, UK.

Teach Yourself ®

The CREATIVE WRITING Workbook

Matthew Branton

First published in Great Britain in 2013 by Hodder & Stoughton. An Hachette UK company.

First published in US in 2013 by The McGraw-Hill Companies, Inc.

Copyright © Matthew Branton 2013

The right of Matthew Branton to be identified as the Author of the Work has been asserted by him in accordance with the Copyright, Designs and Patents Act 1988.

Database right Hodder & Stoughton (makers)

The *Teach Yourself* name is a registered trademark of Hachette UK.

British Library Cataloguing in Publication Data: a catalogue record for this title is available from the British Library.

Library of Congress Catalog Card Number: on file.

10 9 8 7 6 5 4 3 2 1

The publisher has used its best endeavours to ensure that any Website addresses referred to in this book are correct and active at the time of going to press. However, the publisher and the author have no responsibility for the Websites and can make no guarantee that a site will remain live or that the content will remain relevant, decent or appropriate.

The publisher has made every effort to mark as such all words which it believes to be trademarks. The publisher should also like to make it clear that the presence of a word in the book, whether marked or unmarked, in no way affects its legal status as a trademark.

Every reasonable effort has been made by the publisher to trace the copyright holders of material in this book. Any errors or omissions should be notified in writing to the publisher, who will endeavour to rectify the situation for any reprints and future editions.

Cover image © frenta / fotolia

Typeset by Cenveo® Publisher Services.

Printed and bound by CPI Group (UK) Ltd, Croydon, CR0 4YY

Hodder & Stoughton policy is to use papers that are natural, renewable and recyclable products and made from wood grown in sustainable forests. The logging and manufacturing processes are expected to conform to the environmental regulations of the country of origin.

Hodder & Stoughton Ltd

338 Euston Road

London NW1 3BH

www.hodder.co.uk

Acknowledgements

The author and publisher would like to express their thanks for permission to reproduce extracts from the following works:

Wilfred Owen, 'The Last laugh', *Wilfred Owen: The War Poems*, ed. Jon Stallworthy (Chatto & Windus, 1994).

Craig Raine. 'A Martian Sends a Postcard Home', in Craig Raine, *Collected Poems, 1978–1998* (London: Picador, 2000).

George Saunders, 'The End of FIRPO in the World', *Pastoralia* (London: Bloomsbury, 2001).

Every effort has been made to trace the copyright for material used in this book. The authors and publishers would be happy to make arrangements with any holder of copyright whom it has not been possible to trace by the time of going to press.

Contents

How to use this book

Creative writing is good for you:

▶ **It's easy:** we all make observations and create phrases every day

▶ **It's natural:** taking stock of life, and expressing the feelings such thoughts evoke, is a valuable part of being human

▶ **It's healthy:** exploring what makes people tick, or how spring flowers need winter frosts, or any other aspect of life, builds an interesting, rounded, and capable personality.

Creative writers are people who are well versed at both appreciating life with clear eyes, and thinking around its problems. It's the nature of creativity, and its reward.

But, as any budding creative writer will agree, this craft has a steep learning curve. We respect authors because few other disciplines require as much dedicated effort, and such a long apprenticeship, to produce a single artefact – a collection of poems, a memoir or biography, a completed draft of a novel or screenplay. It's a demanding, technical craft.

Yet, like any craft, creative writing has evolved practical solutions to the problem its apprentices must overcome: turning an individual's experience and perspective into words that do it justice. There are many names for this: readability, pace, intrigue; writing that comes alive on the page, which has that elusive page-turning quality.

This book will guide you through exactly how creative writers achieve this X-factor – how they win readers, and do justice to their material – exploring the wide variety of ideas, perspectives and technical tools at a sure-footed writer's disposal. The analysis and original exercises you'll find here will teach you:

▶ How to build a compelling 'voice on the page' in all kinds of creative writing

▶ How to begin to see the world like a writer, and generate striking and original imagery to enhance and augment your creativity

▶ How to get your writing into gear and build page-turning pace into everything you create

▶ How to write description, character and action, with key techniques for authors seeking to maximize scope and impact

▶ How to decide the course of your creative piece to maximize its potential, rather than trusting to inspiration (also known as 'how to defeat writer's block').

We'll examine the concepts and techniques, then try them out in original exercises designed specifically to get you writing, and enjoying the sense of accomplishment and capability that comes with developing, augmenting and enhancing your core creative skills.

I began writing a dozen years before I first saw my name in print, and it was a few years after that before I published my first novel. But in those few years I went from writing for a local listings magazine to writing for a city daily, to writing blurbs and press releases for a publishing house, to freelancing features and interviews to national dailies, to being interviewed myself as a novelist. My writing apprenticeship was lengthy, but once I got going I was on a roll.

Yet I remember those long, blood-from-a-stone years very well, and two things in particular. First, the obstinate refusal of my writing to flow like sinuous mountain stream water – more often, the effect I got was of an outfall grumbling over junked tyres and shopping trolleys. The second problem came when I finally read what I'd written back to myself. Though I could see improvements on the page, things like better imagery and snappier transitions, from project to project, still my writing fell far short of where I wanted it to be.

In my career since I've been fortunate enough to chew the fat with many of my favourite authors and film-makers, and have learned that I really wasn't alone all those years. The gap – the vast yawning gulf, it can seem like – between what you know of good writing from your personal reading, and what you produce on the page, can seem insuperable for a long time, even to the most dedicated creative-writing apprentice.

This is the steep part of the learning curve, and this book will help you up and over it. If you have an idea, but aren't sure how to build a piece around it; if you love to sit down and write, and want to move on from fragments and vignettes to fully fledged pieces; or if you're tackling projects already but find plot, characters or your line-by-line writing itself just won't come alive on the page as they should, this book will help you.

It will help you progress in your writing:

▶ explaining tried-and-tested creative techniques that tackle the problems all budding writers face

▶ sharing the insider tricks and tips that professionals use to inject zest and zing line by line

▶ letting you practise new skills, with fun exercises to get your writing and creativity flowing in ways that you will see and feel straight away.

From creating original imagery to structuring life writing and memoir, from building gripping plot twists and character arcs to creating striking travel writing, this book will share the secrets of poetry, fiction, drama, biography and memoir, and the exciting and fast-moving world of factual writing, to equip you with the key skill sets of creative writing. It will help you find your footing, as you forge ahead in your creativity, with original, guided writing exercises designed to engage and develop your existing skills, wherever you are on your journey as a writer.

This book's original exercises will help you develop your perspectives and talents as a writer, helping you understand and practise each new technique and concept, with plenty of examples and analysis to pin down exactly:

▶ how the primary rule of creative writing – **Show Don't Tell** – frees writers to work with both power and fine nuance in creative pieces, gripping a reader's attention from the first lines

▶ how to 'set the scene' effectively and evocatively in a creative piece, using the contrast between **location** and **milieu** to inject meaning and dimensionality

▶ how creative writers from biographers to novelists make their characters come alive on the page, using **characterization** and developing **deep character**

▶ how **core-value progressions** fuel creative pieces, from powerful opening to resonant conclusion

▶ how to engineer **story progressions** and **character arcs** together, to build meaning, resonance and emotional power in your work

▶ how to create **dimensionality** line by line on the page, crafting your own **original imagery**, turning your **feelings** and **perspectives** into an experience readers can share

▶ how to build **coherent** and **satisfying** creative pieces from single and small-seeming ideas.

This book will help you make that big leap, from thinking about creative writing as an interesting thing to take on, or even making your first voyages on a writer's journey, to feeling sure-footed and confident each time you flex creative muscle. With original exercises designed so that you can see for yourself the techniques in action – using the tools confidently in your own hands – the chapters ahead will teach you how the spectrum of creative writers, from memoirists, biographers and life writers, to poets and novelists and travel writers, achieve their entertaining and intriguing effects on the page.

1

Write now

In this chapter you will learn:
▶ Why writing is the essential skill set of modern life.
▶ Why it's never been a better time to be a writer.
▶ About the key technique of all readable writing, with easy-start exercises to try it for yourself.
▶ How to build interest and intrigue in everything you write.

→ # Writing in the twenty-first century

Despite decades of doomy forecasts, reading and writing are more central to our lives today than ever before. Until recently, most people wrote little more than a shopping list from one week to the next. Work was all about meetings; social life about phone calls and 'face time'. The dedicated few might pen a letter to a loved one occasionally, but few people wrote in the course of everyday life.

Now we do little else. Twenty-first century careers are all about delivering; the days of being 'meat in the room' at meetings are long gone. Now many of us compose detailed writing – presentations or reports that must capture attention and convey complex facts and ideas – as a core part of our everyday employment.

As for our free time, texting, tweeting and social media have given everyone a platform to entertain, to share, to joke or prank. Writing used to be a 'difficult' thing best attempted by experts only: now we all dash off witticisms, and create moments of poetry, or of vivid evocativeness, as part of our everyday interaction with friends and family, and often work colleagues, too. Writing gives us opportunities to share experiences and trade banter, taking traditional human chatting into a new kind of social space.

→ Why we're all writers already

Nowadays many people want to learn to write because they write, text, post and comment online as part of daily life, and find that they enjoy it. But before the digital revolution and its new ways to communicate, writing was a more specialized sphere. If people wanted to learn to write, it was usually because they enjoyed reading, and that's still a big draw for many budding authors.

And recent years have created many new readers, putting books back in the heart of the culture. The 'non-fiction revolution' of the 1990s, when bestsellers like Dava Sobel's *Longitude* and Sebastian Junger's *The Perfect Storm* imported techniques from novels into non-fiction, opened up a whole new world of popular fact-based reading. At the same time, publishing phenomena like Harry Potter or the more recent Scandinavian cop-story craze brought new revenue streams to cash-strapped fiction publishers, freeing them to invest and innovate.

Meanwhile, the online revolution has revitalized the world of magazines and newspapers, creating a new kind of journalism – blogging – that ordinary people often excel at. The world of books and print media has rarely been more vibrant, inspiring more and more people to try their hand at writing what they love to read.

But of course books and other 'old media' are just one part of the world of writing today. Phone messaging, online forums, and the ubiquitous social media provide many platforms for us all to write and be read. Chances are, if you want to tackle the key skills of prose or even poetry, it's because you're writing already and maybe even enjoying it.

Exercise 1

WHERE ARE YOU AS A WRITER?

What kinds of writing do you accomplish already? Rate your enjoyment on a scale of 1 to 5, with a score of 1 for **I do a good job but it's always a job** and a score of 5 for the writing that can sometimes seem to flow from your fingertips:

→ I write reports and presentations for my job ☐

→ I've written a speech (e.g. for a wedding or family event) ☐

→ I keep up with friends on social media sites or text/tweet socially ☐

→ I've tried my hand at writing:

family history, or biography ☐

life writing or memoir ☐

fiction ☐

poetry ☐

drama ☐

journalism ☐

→ I keep a blog, journal or diary ☐

→ I post or comment online ☐

So how did you rate?

If much of the writing you enjoy is online, then you'll know you're not alone. Social media is where the phrase makers of tomorrow cut their teeth today. Banter that was once the domain of the coffee break or beers with friends can be shared and enjoyed with anyone any time, thanks to social media. As with writing wedding speeches, or a humorous eulogy for a colleague's leaving party, social writing prizes wit, using quick-fire set-ups to deliver a punchline payload. If telling anecdotes, swapping banter, or making humorous speeches is what got you interested in writing, this book will show you how to build on your skills and take them further.

Storytelling is for many an innate human skill. Maybe your adventures in narrative have begun – as for many writers – by telling stories at parties or with friends, and realizing you have a knack for it. Or maybe you've already begun to put narratives together, for humorous effect online, or showcasing your work on a flash-fiction site – or equally in reports and presentations at work – and found you've enjoyed the process. Perhaps, inspired by authors you admire, you've turned your hand to attempting a short story or vignette. Or maybe you're a first-time author attempting a novel of your own. This book will help you explore the key skills of storytelling, and exercise them yourself to take your fiction to the next level.

Life writing, which can encompass family history, memoir and biography, uses tools from all kinds of prose writing. To make their subjects come alive, life writers use techniques to build character, location, mood and drama just as storytellers like novelists and screenwriters do. Memoir and fact-based non-fiction draw readers into their stories by using many of the techniques of both storytelling and journalism. The striking imagery of poetry is another key skill of life writing, deployed to deliver the essence of distant people, places and times.

Poetry is for some an art form unto itself, but almost all successful poetry uses techniques from across the spectrum of page-turning writing, to create intrigue and interest. As we'll see, poems can use exactly the same strategies as factual writing, like journalism or memoir and life writing, or even fiction, to draw a reader into a piece and get them engaged with it. We'll break these techniques down and practise them on the page, to get at their essence – that ongoing spark of intrigue that keeps a reader captivated.

→ The essence of creative writing

Whatever kind of creative writing you want to accomplish, be it poetry or autobiography, drama or fiction, you'll be working with the same basic material: words on a page.

Every artistic medium has its own limitations. Sculptors are bound by the laws of physics and molecular structure. Painters, and even photographers, must artificially replicate the light upon which their vision of the world depends. Writers, whether they publish online or on paper, must work with nothing more than characters and blank space.

But limitations tend to create opportunities in life: tennis would be a dull game with no net. Similarly, the history of painting, from cave wall to gallery wall to subway, wouldn't be half so interesting if artists weren't constantly striving against the technical limitations of the paints and pigments available. So it is with creative writing. The sheer limitation of having nothing but monochrome ink on a page for expression has itself created one of the most engaging experiences in our culture. Because, when readers are doing their thing, they give it their whole attention. Even when checking our messages, when we read we are entirely focused on interpreting what we're seeing. Some kinds of writing, like novels and poetry, even encourage their readers to find a quiet space, all the more to focus solely on the experience. This intensity of focus gives writers special opportunities to connect with their audience, which every kind of writing has evolved to exploit according to its own characteristics.

WHAT DO YOU VALUE AS A READER?

These questions apply to all the reading you do, from work reading and newspapers to messaging friends or chatting online. Again, rate these 1 to 5.

→ **Interest** – writing which provokes intellectual curiosity, and gets you thinking ☐

→ **Engrossment** – when the author engages both your interest and your emotional involvement ☐

→ **Wit** – where a humorous perspective is delivered using creative-writing techniques such as 'set-up and pay-off' ☐

→ **Aesthetic engagement** – where descriptive or poetic writing moves the human faculty for appreciation and awe ☐

→ **Drama** – an unfolding story that grabs your attention, making you read on to find out what happens ☐

If you're like most readers, you'll appreciate a few of the above. They're qualities that all kinds of authors, from journalists to poets to hardboiled thriller writers, build into their writing to get a reader hooked and turning pages. As we move through this workbook, we'll explore the strategies authors use to create engrossing, engaging writing, and try out the professional techniques that inject interest, pace and drama into everything from news reports to literary novels.

→ Building intrigue

But first, let's focus on the very essence of all creative writing: **It must hook a reader. It must secure their attention. It needs to leave them in no doubt that, of all the other things they could be doing right now, reading on is the best choice.**

All budding writers realize this, but many mistake what it means. Some think it means that they must use fancy or unusual words, to get a reader's interest. Others think it means that lots of ornate description is necessary, to help a reader 'see' what they're writing about. Some think it means using extremes of action or expression, to force involvement; others go for the opposite approach, grounding what they write so thoroughly in the everyday – the calm before the storm of their narratives – that their pieces are too weighted down to fly.

Which isn't to say that there isn't a place for ornate description, unusual diction, the extreme or the everyday in creative writing. Each can add their own kind of value for a reader. But to *build* that elusive, page-turning quality into a piece of writing from the start, an author must create intrigue.

Engaging writing creates intrigue, before it does anything else. It gives the reader a reason to read on, often in the very first line.

Here's the opening sentence of T. S. Eliot's famous poem *The Waste Land*:

> *April is the cruellest month, breeding*
> *Lilacs out of the dead land, mixing*
> *Memory and desire, stirring*
> *Dull roots with spring rain.*
>
> (Selected Poems of T. S. Eliot, 2002)

A cheerful response to the passing of winter is one of the most basic animal traits. It's something we feel in ourselves each spring – and hear in the birdsong, see it in the skipping lambs and mad March hares. Poems about spring tend to celebrate the rising of the sap.

But in this poem spring is a torment. The rising of the life force is 'cruel', even as we hear its relentless insistence in those pulsing verbs ('breeding', 'mixing', 'stirring'). The opening two words create the set-up expectation – *April is…* – these could be from a musical, with a young swain about to burst into song. But then the expectation is abruptly turned back – 'April is the cruellest month' – and three striking images in succession drive this unexpected twist home.

Similarly, this is the first line of George Orwell's novel *Nineteen Eighty-Four*:

> *It was a bright cold day in April and the clocks were striking thirteen.*

Orwell wrote and published his classic novel just after World War II – so readers tackling that first line have always known that this April day is in the future. The surprise at the end of the sentence ('clocks ... striking thirteen') confirms, then, what we already know. The *intrigue*, however, is built into those first few words – it's cold, in this future.

It's a big surprise, and a visceral one. Up until Orwell's novel, writing about the future was mostly propaganda for progress. The future would be a wonderful place, of course, where robots would do all the work while we breeze about in jet-cars. But in Orwell's future something as simple as whether or not it's cold out still matters to people – and so it proves, in Winston Smith's dingy world of dank tenements, scant food and threadbare survival.

TWISTS: HOW TO INJECT INTRIGUE

Intrigue is generated in both the poem and the novel above by leading the reader's expectation one way – it's spring! It's the future! – and then subverting that expectation.

In *The Waste Land*, regeneration in the warmth of spring is painful; the restoration of feeling to frozen limbs is 'cruel'. These assertions are the opposite of what we expect, when the subject is springtime. Similarly, in the future world of *Nineteen Eighty-Four*, the progress we expect in human society simply hasn't happened – the mass of people still shiver in the wind. In both literary classics, expectation is invoked then subverted in the very first sentence. Writers call this technique, creating expectation then turning it around, a reversal, or 'twist'.

Exercise 3

INTRIGUE IN ACTION – 'TWISTS'

Consider the following scenario:

A body is found on a riverbank after a storm. It's in the middle of a flurry of muddy footprints; it has leaked blood into the mud beneath it, and the clothes and exposed skin are caked in mud. If you were writing this story, which of these developments would you choose?

→ The victim turns out to be alive, but in a permanent coma.

→ The victim turns out to be an alien, killed to silence his warning of intergalactic chaos.

→ The victim turns out to have died before the rain fell, when the ground was baked dry.

So which of these three plot twists did you feel promised the most intriguing story? Unless you're a big *Dr Who* fan, you probably picked the third option. It opens up intriguing new ground for the story, feeding the reader the very first clues regarding whodunit. The chase is on.

HOW TWISTS WORK

Reversals are something that all page-turning writing uses, as a basic building block. An expectation is created; then something unexpected happens. Consider a newspaper article, an interview with someone who's survived a tragedy. The first lines of the piece might run something like:

> *Butterflies flutter among the neat gardens of Primrose Terrace. The sound of children playing in a neighbourhood park drifts over the trim, tidy houses. But at number 32, windows are shut tight against the breeze and the garden gate is bolted.*

It's such a familiar technique that we expect it – and if it's not there in a piece of writing, we notice. If an initial expectation isn't invoked then intriguingly subverted, we don't feel 'pulled in' as we read.

Sometimes this manoeuvre is accomplished in the first line of a piece of writing, and sometimes it's built gradually. Short stories often use a fast set-up, but in Raymond Carver's acclaimed story 'Cathedral' a chatty opening passage takes a couple of pages. The narrator tells us of an impending visit by an old friend of his wife's – a blind man, her intimate confidant for many years. The wife and the blind guy sound nice, but the narrator briskly reveals himself to be a sour kind of guy, insecure and jealous. Yet his voice is refreshing in its frankness, and the way he talks about his own insecurities and personal failures is amusing. We kind of like the guy, even as we roll our eyes at some of what he's saying. This tension makes us read on, intrigued, to see how this guy messes up the weekend – or not, because we know that expectations stories create with their openings are rarely how it turns out.

In William Golding's classic novel *Lord of the Flies* the action opens with a schoolboy scrambling over rocks in the seaside sun. We think we know what's going on, as we read the first paragraphs. But when the boy leaves the beach for the jungle behind it, the terrible truth dawns – there are many kids here, stranded alone on a desert island after a plane crash. If the author had started with the obvious opening – the full-on, heart-in-mouth terror of a plane going down – his readers may have felt they'd seen this scene before, in many classic movies. Instead, Golding opted for intrigue over graphic action in his opening, and created an opening 'hook' that's all the more gripping.

Robert Frost's classic poem 'Stopping by Woods on a Snowy Evening' similarly uses intrigue to pull us into the world of the writing. The opening stanza tells us little more than the title, but with a couple of intriguing spin-shots in its four clauses:

> *Whose woods these are I think I know.*
> *His house is in the village though;*
> *He will not mind me stopping here*
> *To watch his woods fill up with snow.*
>
> (Robert Frost's Poems, 2002)

There's something strange going on, we realize. Something clandestine, possibly even dangerous. The simple, incantatory rhythm and soft sounds echo the snow falling – but make it sound like the speaker is getting sleepy, too. Stopping to watch snow fall in darkening woods, far from human habitation, seems a bad call for this person by the end of the first stanza; the second stanza shows us that the speaker knows this, but is doing it anyway.

But, as the poem moves briskly through its deceptively simple lines, we realize that the 'sleepiness' set up in the first lines is metaphorical as well as literal. In the fourth stanza the speaker snaps out of this snow-induced reverie and rides on, accepting that there are 'miles to go before I sleep'. Intriguing 'scene-setting' in this poem's opening lines is used to hook us into reading about Death, a natural subject for art but one that we naturally find difficult to consider.

Exercise 4

BUILDING INTRIGUE

All writing needs to 'set a scene' and draw the reader into it. From crime reporters covering grisly murders to poets celebrating life, writers need to get a reader into the world of their piece, and intrigued enough to read on.

So let's try some 'opening lines' writing. Take 15 minutes for this exercise. Write two paragraphs (if you're a poet, two stanzas) that zoom in on a bowl of fruit in an empty room. The location of the room, the quantity and kind of fruit, the condition of the building or the produce, present day or distant past – these are all up to you. All you have to do is create some intrigue along the way.

_____

_____

_____

_____

_____

_____

_____

_____

_____

_____

_____

_____

_____

_____

_____

_____

_____

_____

So how did you do? Maybe you created a room shrouded in mourning-cloth and cobwebs, but with fresh vivid fruit in the bowl – or maybe your room was spanking-clean, with everything hi-tech and up to the minute, but the fruit in the bowl was shrivelled and flyblown. Maybe it was a dingy room, with scant furnishings or comforts but plums with the blush of summer warming the space; or maybe a room full of luxury and plenty, with an exquisite crystal bowl containing a few sour grapes. Maybe your room was in a far-off land, with fruity treats that Western palates would find beyond challenging. Or maybe it was an all-American room, full of buckskin nostalgia and patriotic knick-knacks, but with ripe reeking durian fruit in the bowl.

 Exercise 5

PACE AND POWER

Now boil your fruit bowl piece down. If you're a prose writer, turn your two paragraphs into two sentences. If you're a poet, condense your two stanzas into a haiku.

_____

_____

_____

_____

Whatever the fruit bowl scenario you created, by now you should have something that creates an expectation in the reader then tweaks interest by subverting it. You'll have spent the first half of each of your exercise pieces on set-up – the what, where and when of your scenario, manipulating these variables to create an expectation. You then subverted this constructed expectation with the 'pay-off', slingshotting your scenario forward with intrigue. (If you feel this didn't happen for you yet, try these exercises again with a candlestick or a vase of flowers, and one of the scenarios I've listed between Exercises 4 and 5.)

Where to next?

This technique of set-up and pay-off in line-by-line writing is what we'll take forward into the next chapter, discovering how writers use it to add that page-turning quality to everything from blog pieces to poems, from newspaper features to plays and novels. As we begin writing about places and people, we'll practise using carefully chosen detail and colour to build **set-up and pay-off**, bringing situations and locations alive on the page.

Ideas and inspirations

▶ Our fast-paced technology and culture create ever-new opportunities for writers, from tweeting as art form to 'flash fiction' to a renewed appreciation for books. There's never been a better time to be a writer.

▶ Novice writers are rare these days. Most of us write creatively as part of our daily routine, be it leisure, family time or work.

▶ Taking creative writing further means building on the skills we use when we message each other on our phones, or post and chat online, or tell anecdotes, or write reports.

▶ The core skills of writing – which make good poets and good novelists, good journalists and dramatists and memoirists – are the same skills because they use the same basic material: words on a page.

▶ Using simple techniques of set-up and pay-off, to create interest and intrigue, brings that elusive, page-turning quality to everything we write.

2 Setting the scene

· ·

In this chapter you will learn:

▶ How to create the 'world' of your piece on the page.

▶ Professional techniques for setting the scene in your writing.

▶ About location and milieu, and how to use them together to make the setting of a creative piece come alive for a reader.

▶ Practical ways to begin combining the natural flow of your writing with helpful techniques.

· ·

As we saw in the last chapter, creative writers use techniques of set-up and pay-off throughout their work – not just for creating action and plot, but often in their very first lines. We analysed how writers like George Orwell and T. S. Eliot powered the openings of their masterpieces with 'hook line' first sentences, using surprise and intrigue to help readers engage with their writing and enter their created worlds.

It's this engagement that brings reader and author into a collaborative mental space. In everyday terms, people call this effect 'page-turning reading'. It's that unmistakable immersion in words alone – becoming 'lost' in a piece of writing – that is the prize of a creative author's endeavour.

→ Beginning with the beginning: What opening lines need

All creative pieces must 'set the scene'. The basics of **when, where, who** and **what** must be supplied to the reader – *Long ago, in a kingdom far away, a knight rode out to rescue a princess.*

The convention is so deeply ingrained in us, from nursery stories onward, that it's easy to forget that each of these variables – who, what, where, when – are equally fruitful tools for creating reader engagement and story. Naturally, new writers focus on the two monoliths – who and what – and let where and when flow from these, as just a couple of boxes to be ticked in the necessary groundwork of a piece's opening movement.

Experienced writers, however, use when and where as two more tools to create story.

For some, this permits brevity – setting up when and where as economically as possible, to pitch the reader directly into the action with scene-setting keywords:

> *The lunch crowd at Za-Za's was strictly Botox and big rocks.*

For others, when and where can be used to establish mood and theme, often symbolically:

> *A rat ran under reeking dumpsters and along a grimy alley then, turning sharp into bright sunshine, skittered between thousand-dollar shoes as they stepped through Za-Za's discreet doorway, and disappeared into the tastefully ambient shadows inside.*

Another author might approach the question of where and when by 'going deep', following a wealthy customer – or a kitchen porter – as they prepare for lunch at Za-Za's. Intrigue can be created with such deep set-up, showing a glamorous heiress with a perfect life cooking prescription drugs to keep her topped-up through lunch, or an ICU nurse emerging from a night's life-or-death drama and swapping her scrubs for a dishwasher's whites. Neither of these characters may prove to be the who of the piece, but this deep set-up approach roots creative narrative in its where and when.

Exercise 6

SETTING THE SCENE

Look at the three examples of scene-setting approaches above, whose *where* is a restaurant named Za-Za's at lunchtime, and try to locate the *when* of each. You should find each with a little careful combing.

▶ In the brief, hit-the-ground running approach, *when* is established by 'Botox'.

▶ In the symbolic, mood-setting approach, *when* is established by 'thousand-dollar shoes'.

▶ In the deep set-up approaches, the *whens* are in 'ICU' and 'cooking prescription drugs'.

As you can see, these *when* variables are chosen carefully. Swap 'Botox' for 'facelifts' and the when could be 50 years ago. Swap 'thousand-dollar shoes' for hundred-dollar and ditto. Swap prescription drugs for Martinis and it's the mid-twentieth century again; substitute vodka and the setting is more recent – but the precise choice used locates the action firmly in the era of oxy and vikes.

You'll also have noticed, as you analysed each example, that the where in each – Za-Za's restaurant – is 'spun' by the when. The two variables work in conjunction with each other to set the scene in two ways. It's set literally, in that we're told when and where the focus of this piece of writing is trained – where the action or theme of the piece is to play out.

Finally, you'll have noticed that there's 'scene-setting' going on, too: the references to Botox, the rat, the heiress's little helper, and the nurse paying off her tuition all prepare us to read on in a very particular way. This expectation, created in the reader with a few deft words, can now be teased out and exploited, or subverted and turned around entirely by an author in command of their material.

This authority begins by exploiting all the choices open to an author with a blank page before them, so let's try working the when and where of a fresh scenario to both establish and slingshot a creative piece forward.

Exercise 7

WHO AND WHAT, WHEN AND WHERE

Choose one of the following:

→ A gunboat loading ammo at a dock

→ The last day of term at an exclusive college

→ An attractive intern's first after-work drink with colleagues, who are all mid-life members of the opposite sex.

 Now choose a when and a where for your scenario. The gunboat could be anywhere from the American Civil War to Vietnam to the liquid-methane floodplains of a far-flung intergalactic battle zone. The fancy college could be in Vienna in Freud's day, or Beverley Hills in Paris Hilton's. The intern could be a woman on a fishing boat in 1918, or a young man in an office where *Twilight* and *Fifty Shades of Grey* were the book club's last picks.

_____

_____

_____

_____

With your when and where choices made, now try to work these variables together to create your scenario on the page. First, try the fast, economical approach – try to establish when and where, and get some friction going between the two, in one or two lines at most. If you're flummoxed, go back to the 'Botox' example in the previous exercise, and think about how it painted overtones into establishing lunchtime at Za-Za's.

_____

_____

_____

_____

_____

_____

Next try the symbolic approach with your scenario, then sketch out
a deep set-up approach. If you find progress thorny, look for fruit
in the contrast between your chosen scenario and the rest of the
world continuing around it.

_____

_____

_____

_____

_____

_____

_____

_____

_____

_____

_____

_____

_____

_____

→ Scene-setting: Location and milieu

Creative writing makes good use of every available variable. The setting of a creative piece can be described in a few words or a few pages, but two elements will always be in place:

1 The **location** of the scene in physical space and time

2 The **milieu**

The latter looks like a scary technical term but it's something we've already worked with in the last exercise. Milieu is the set of social, economic and/or cultural factors that define the location, and thereby create expectation in the reader. To return to Za-Za's a moment, 'Botox and big rocks' – and 'thousand-dollar shoes' sharing space with stinking dumpsters and rats – spin the location of the restaurant with loaded information about its clientele.

That loaded information creates expectation about what's to come, which a skilful author can then subvert with a twist. For example, the Za-Za's set-up could preface a scene in which a down-and-out disowned child begs for help from a wealthy parent, or vice versa – only for our sympathies to be twisted exquisitely with each revelation of the action.

Milieu makes the setting of a creative piece come alive on the page. It's with milieu that authors begin the process of building meaning into their writing. Let's try another exercise, before we look at some classic examples.

 *Exercise 8*

MILIEU AND SETTING

In Philip Larkin's poem 'MCMXIV' three of the four stanzas build a beautiful description of Britain and its people in late summer. Yet they show a season long past: the first stanza speaks of men with caps and moustaches gathered in orderly lines outdoors, as if queuing for a big cricket match; the second stanza pans to the world around the men – dusty summertime streets with children playing, old-fashioned shops with tin adverts for products of yesteryear nailed up outside; the penultimate stanza moves out of the town to the heat-hazed countryside beyond.

It's a lovely sequence of verses a pastoral idyll that might make any British person long for home, and perhaps for a time past, too. This is the location of the creative piece, its focus in physical space. The final stanza brings the milieu, which makes us recast the emotion evoked by the poem's first image – the men queuing are signing up to fight, in 1914. This innocent world will never be the same again.

For this exercise, choose a historical event that moves you. It could be 9/11; it could be the Moon landing; it could be the day Anne Frank began her diary. Write a paragraph setting the scene, and build it toward a milieu-setting last line. Google the full text of Larkin's poem if you're stuck. When you're satisfied, try rewriting your first line to link to the last – thematically, rhythmically, with a first-line set-up and a last-line pay-off... the choice is yours.

_____

_____

_____

_____

_____

_____

_____

_____

_____

_____

_____

_____

_____

_____

→ Two case studies: Location and Milieu

I KNOW WHY THE CAGED BIRD SINGS BY MAYA ANGELOU

The opening to this remarkable work of autobiography pitches the reader directly into a crowded church in the American Deep South, where the protagonist, a young girl, is stuttering over a poem on stage. The verse is a silly rhyming couplet intended to sound cute for the event, Easter Sunday, but the speaker can't get beyond its first cloying clauses.

The where, who and what are swiftly established with beautifully constructed yet simple opening lines. The milieu is established when, stuck in her stutter and unable to bear the shameful glare of the congregation, the little girl retreats into her own head. There, we learn of how hopeful she'd been when her mother sewed her frock for the occasion, a dress so special that the little girl fantasized that people would see the beauty within her when she wore it.

Milieu is established movingly yet with precision in this sequence. Swiftly we learn:

▶ that the little girl is black, though she longs for blonde hair, and not having to cake Vaseline and red dirt on her legs to lighten her skin tone for 'Sunday best'

▶ that her special dress is a cut-down handout from a white woman.

Angelou is working with powerful sensual material here. We can feel how unpleasant it would be to smear Vaseline and mud on your skin before putting on your good clothes. We can see how a wealthy woman's cut-down frock would make a poor little girl look ridiculous, and emphasize her status at the bottom of a segregated society. The pitiful cosmetics she uses – toxic hair straighteners, along with the mud mixture – are endured by the protagonist as if her body is somehow wrong, emphasizing the inhuman racist nature of the power balance in her world.

The power of this opening situation is redoubled when the milieu is introduced, bringing meaning to the scene-setting with the special information that the milieu carries. Angelou takes a lot of risks here: the opening lines consist of the staccato stuttering of the mystifying doggerel, before the author abruptly fractures the chronology with a flashback. This segues into intense an interior monologue, before returning to the excruciating present, where the heroine is forced to run out of church as her bladder betrays her.

This all happens in a brief prologue, before the first chapter, but the powerful project of an extraordinary autobiography is set up by this pacey, intense establishment of location and milieu. Angelou's story is of childhood sexual abuse and rape, followed by the little girl's uncles beating the rapist to death. The little girl who stuttered in church then withdraws into herself, becoming near-mute for many years, overcome by the consequences both of rape and of speaking out; her gradual recovery is a story of courage and human dignity in the inhuman world of American apartheid.

Angelou's book is also a virtuoso demonstration of technical accomplishment, which millions of readers worldwide revere as one of the great works of American literature. Its depth and complexity are set up in this deft opening sequence, with the little girl's experience in church foreshadowing the burdens of guilt and shame that the story will see her forced to shoulder. In this remarkable opening sequence, as through the crises of the story yet to come, the burdened little girl must retreat into her core self to escape, prefiguring the terrible impact of what happens next.

Angelou brings meaning and impact to her story, from its first lines, by establishing the milieu – the inhumanity of the segregated South. The little girl's gradual recovery from terrible traumas, making bootstrap decisions for herself, out of the least privileged place in society, is a powerful story of human survival and a powerful indictment of the abuse of power. Angelou's technical skill, as a writer willing to take risks and make them work on the page, carries an extraordinary, ground-breaking piece of life writing.

 Exercise 9

DETAIL AND COLOUR

Fuelling an opening scene where location, milieu and action work together to create dimensionality and meaning calls for keen observation skills, to equip you with everyday colour and detail to cherry-pick for your writing. In coming exercises we'll look at how to find new ways of seeing, and get ideas for your writing, out in the world, but first we'll journey into the colour of your mind's eye.

Think of a place you particularly enjoyed living. It might be a childhood home; it might be the first place you chose as your own. Now perch on a high rooftop and take a bird's-eye view. What are the first six things you notice from such a vantage? What are the landmarks, the hubs of activity, the telling details that catch your eye? Listen to the Beatles' song 'Penny Lane' if freeing your narrative eye doesn't come easily.

_____

_____

_____

_____

_____

_____

_____

_____

_____

_____

_____

Now use the things you've picked out to create a little world. Write a few short paragraphs linking each detail you picked up on, but try not to use a single character pottering from one location to the next. Perhaps a certain time of day could invoke a chain of routine actions through the neighbourhood, or a weather event – like sudden rain turning to pelting hail – could trigger a Mexican wave of sudden scurrying activity.

_____

_____

_____

_____

_____

_____

_____

_____

_____

_____

_____

_____

_____

_____

_____

_____

_____

If you found satisfaction in this exercise, then there's real cause for celebration. You've just created a world, probably distant in time and place from where you are now, beginning with nothing but a few visual details. You've picked out what makes that particular world tick, and breathed life into it on the page.

We'll explore the sure-fire way to defeat 'writer's block' at the end of this chapter, but whenever you feel stuck, or that your mojo isn't quite working, return to this exercise and rerun it with different variables – a snowfall or ice storm, a burst water main or a crushing heatwave. Using your own memories and experiences to generate flow in your writing for a moment, before you focus your attention on the project in hand, can be a reliable and practical way to limber up when you sit down to write. Scene-setting, with milieu bringing local colour to life, is a high-octane business, even in pastoral verse: now, let's look at another example of location quickened with milieu, from another classic author.

'THE DARKLING THRUSH' BY THOMAS HARDY

The location of this famous poem is a countryside stile on a frozen winter afternoon, with the shadows lengthening and sun fading. The milieu is supplied with imagery – the speaker likens the ridges and shadows of the barren winter landscape to 'the Century's corpse', and the keening of the wind to 'its death-lament'. This exact moment, we realize, is the last fading of the sun on the last day of the nineteenth century. It's easy to imagine Hardy, bundled up in a poacher's coat with his breath pluming in the air, as he strode out that afternoon himself.

But the poem tells us nothing about its speaker, except what we can glean from the choices of imagery used. It's the milieu of the poem – the last hours of an epochal century, with all the associations our culture ascribes to such occasions – that makes the images coalesce into meaning and emotional resonance. Here is the first half of the poem, establishing the location, and introducing the milieu:

I leant upon a coppice gate
When Frost was spectre-grey
And Winter's dregs made desolate
The weakening eye of day.
The tangled bine-stems scored the sky
Like strings of broken lyres
And all mankind that haunted nigh
Had sought their household fires.

The land's sharp features seemed to be
The Century's corpse outleant,
His crypt the cloudy canopy
The wind his death-lament.

The ancient pulse of germ and birth
Was shrunken hard and dry
And every spirit upon earth
Seemed fervourless as I.

The depth of winter is a spiritual ebb for the speaker. His neighbours, possibly his own family, are gathered around warm hearthsides while he's out in a sharp wind conjuring gloomy metaphors.

But the introduction of the milieu – the specific information that spins the setting of a creative piece – tells us that this speaker is more than just a bit emotional. The date, established in the first four lines of the second stanza, carries the entire milieu. It's natural for a thinking person to use 'milestones' like a new century's eve as opportunities to pause in the business of life, and reflect.

And a thinking man, on New Year's Eve in 1899, mightn't have a good deal to be cheerful about. The century's artistic endeavour had been one long revolt against industrialization and dehumanization, from Blake's 'dark Satanic mills' through Dickens' slums and sweatshops, to Conrad's vision of "the horror" at the heart of human exploitation in his extraordinarily prescient 1899 novella *Heart of Darkness*.

Meanwhile, the vigour and variety of such exploitation had burgeoned as never before through the century, with the dual consequences of World War I and the Great Depression waiting in the wings. Hardy's century, which began with hopes of an enlightenment, a new era of human understanding and co-operation, had ended with the masses in slums while the few gorged in absurd luxury.

This is the milieu of Hardy's poem: the state of human affairs at this epochal century's twilight. The speaker's imagery builds around a beautiful central simile – the tangled, dead vegetation resembling 'the strings of broken lyres'. Anyone who's visited an English wood in winter, and seen Pete Townsend in action at a Who concert, can testify that smashed-up guitars with haywire broken strings is indeed a fine description of a British bramble copse after winter storms have blown through.

Hardy probably hadn't seen many smashed guitars, but the lyres he's referencing carry meaning – lyres in literature symbolize arcadia and summer, and time for recreation and culture and good times generally. Hardy's lyres are broken. The golden time is past, maybe never to return. Such seems the speaker's state of mind (or, perhaps, state of soul) at the halfway point of the poem.

It's a lot to build into some brief, gently rhyming lines, and especially to do so without making the speaker sound self-indulgent. The author achieves a big turnaround across the two stanzas:

- In the first stanza, our sympathies lie with the rest of humankind, who have made the sensible decision to retire to their firesides rather than brooding in the dusk.

- In the second stanza, we understand the speaker's decision better – this particular sunset is an epochal moment, and life passes too quickly not to seize on such occasions to reflect on life and one's place in the universe.

This turnaround in our sympathies and strength of identification with the narrator is achieved by establishing location, with some beautifully accurate if gloomy imagery to flesh out the scene, *then* adding meaning to the location by revealing the milieu – we're inside a thinking man's head, taking stock of life at a meaningful juncture in human history, at the end of the most transformative century humankind had yet seen. In Hardy's reflection on this epochal moment, milieu is used to bring meaning to the location of the poem in time and space – setting up the final two stanzas, which contain the action of the poem and its movingly bittersweet resolution.

SCENE-SETTING – WORKING WITH YOUR READER

The act of producing meaning from a creative piece is a collaborative effort between author and reader. When an author sets a scene, the choices he or she makes about what to include and what to leave out are a code that the reader interprets to create meaning.

In this exercise, we'll try some quick-fire scene-setting. Imagine a foggy winter's night, a real peasouper. Try lighting the fog with each of the following in a sentence or two:

→ Streetlamps 20 yards apart

→ Neon

→ Police strobes, which could be in an inner-city crack alley or leafy suburbs.

_____

_____

_____

_____

_____

_____

_____

_____

_____

_____

_____

_____

_____

_____

_____

_____

_____

_____

Now write down the mood you've evoked in each of your three scenarios. There are no right or wrong answers to this exercise. Feel the natural flow of your writing and let it take you where it wants to. If you're stuck, open up the possibilities: the neon could be above a theatrical mecca or a high-class boutique as much as a seedy dive; the flickering police strobes could be lighting a takedown in an inner-city crack alley, or delivering news of an accident to a family home.

_____

_____

_____

_____

_____

_____

_____

_____

_____

_____

_____

_____

_____

_____

Now try these questions:

1. If you were a reader coming to your sketches afresh, what kind of story would each of your scenarios lead you to expect?

2. As the author, what kind of story does each of your sketches make you want to write?

_____

_____

_____

_____

_____

_____

_____

_____

_____

Where to next?

We've covered a lot of ground already, and if you've been able to give time to the exercises so far, then you may well have begun to find your writing groove as your natural flow and the thinking you're doing come together.

But I remember from my own apprenticeship as a writer that the first big achievement is to achieve a natural flow to what you're putting on the page. Combining that natural flow with technical thinking can seem nigh-on impossible when you're struggling just to get one word to follow another. Practice is the key, and working through the exercises in this book will help you get your mojo working.

Writer's block is a much-bemoaned affliction, but defeating writer's block is all about being able to return to your writing headspace each time you can grab an hour or two for work. Excelling as a writer, and capitalizing on all the time and effort you've put in along the way, is about making 'the zone' yours.

Mastering a craft, with all its tools and techniques, is what makes the zone feel like your natural habitat. Far from needing to 'get into' the zone, a trained creative writer inhabits it. The act of sitting down to write transitions a confident craftsperson from the everyday world to the special world of their creativity.

In the coming chapters we'll map this territory, making the tools writers need to thrive in it, and practising the skills to use them. We'll start with the basic building block: a voice on a page. From fourth-wall realism to unreliable narrators, we'll explore the tools and perspectives that help creative authors make confident choices about narrative position and technique in their work.

Ideas and inspirations

▶ Who, what, where, and when are choices creative authors can maximize individually or all together in their writing.

▶ Creative pieces flower into life when meaning is brought to location by milieu.

▶ Authors can use scene-setting to create engagement with readers, working with them to evoke mood, expectation and emotion.

▶ Writers' block is when you become your own harshest critic, and lose your creative footing. It's natural to experience it, but creative writers who gain confidence in their abilities through practice will always have skill sets to rely on when inspiration falters.

3 *Building a voice on the page*

In this chapter you will learn:

▶ How to build a 'voice on the page' in all kinds of creative writing.
▶ About the role of the narrator, and choices and techniques for authors to exploit.
▶ How to use the golden rule of creative writing – Show, Don't Tell – to involve your readers and keep them turning pages.
▶ How action is generated by an author's choices, rather than 'flowing from inspiration'.

→ The scope of the narrator

All creative writing features at least one character, often many. Fiction is fuelled by heroes and villains, protagonists and antagonists, as is stage or screen drama; non-fiction tells stories of human endeavour and diversity, whether the subject is human (as in biography or memoir), or the entire spectrum of existence, as in travel writing. Even a poem that focuses on a pebble and nothing else has a pivotal central character – the narrator.

The job description for a narrator in a creative piece is to act as liaison officer between reader and writer. A narrator is a consciousness, constructed on the page, who mediates the subject of the piece. The narrator is the 'teller of the tale', whether the tale is a poem about a pebble, a travel piece that doesn't deploy a single first-person pronoun, or a three-act play without dialogue.

But a narrator is not just the author's voice. A creative author constructs a purpose-built narrator for each project he or she takes on.

So a narrator can be:

▶ **a character involved in the story** – as in Donna Tartt's classic thriller *The Secret History* or Sylvia Plath's renowned poem 'Lady Lazarus'

▶ **a voice on the page** – as in Joseph Conrad's seminal novel *Heart of Darkness* or Seamus Heaney's much-loved poem 'The Shipping Forecast'.

In drama for stage or screen, which rarely uses an overarching 'voice', the narrator's role is as controller of the created world – the one who makes us discuss the author as much as the actors afterwards. In much popular publishing, fiction or otherwise, the narrator is either right up on the page or firmly in the background; the same is true of both literary fiction and non-fiction.

Narrative scope in creative writing is a broad creative spectrum. Finding your own narrative voice, for each new creative piece you take on, can prove to be complicated work when you're starting out. Lucky beginners can 'hear' their narrators straight off the bat, but for most of us it takes sharp creative thinking.

Putting together a confidently handled 'voice' on the page, which can fully exploit the opportunities of our chosen piece, is a thoughtful but creatively rewarding process. Designing initial narrative choices in order to maximize a piece's natural strengths sets an author in very good stead for the journey ahead.

Exercise 11

WHICH NARRATOR FOR WHICH PROJECT?

Creating a narrator to fit the needs of your writing means making crucial creative choices before you begin putting words on the page. This exercise will take you through some of the choice-making processes writers use as they generate, sift and develop ideas.

1. What qualities does a first-person narrator permit that you enjoy when you read? Rate the following 1 to 5 in order of importance to you.

→ **Immediacy** – hands-on access to the world of the piece means less wordiness ☐

→ **Intimacy** – situations and feelings described from an individual perspective □

→ **Pace** – a first-person narrator can get right into the telling □

→ **Surprise** – a first-person narrator can really make us sit up, as when it turns out they've been feeding us a line (think of the movie *The Usual Suspects* or Zoë Heller's novel *Notes on a Scandal*) □

→ **Emotional power** – experienced first-hand, the emotional world of a story is accessible to a reader with depth and nuance □

Your answers should reveal some of the things you value when you read, and which you may well value developing in your own writing. Surfers talk of having a 'quiver' of boards for different sea conditions – the analogy is to an archer's quiver of arrows. Your responses to the question above represent some of the raw materials you'll use in constructing your own quiver of creative writing strategies.

So let's start to work with them:

2. What positive qualities can a third-person narrator bring to a creative piece? Rate the following from 1 to 5, as above:

→ **Objectivity** – a third-person narrator can give us the big picture, rather than a first-person view □

→ **Detachment** – emotional distance can be maintained, to let readers experience things 'spontaneously' □

→ **Editorial advantage** – a third-person narrator isn't confined to what they experienced personally, and can make creative decisions about what we see and don't see □

→ **Breadth and depth of access** – a roving narrator can follow different subjects intimately or cursorily, sequentially or simultaneously □

→ **Descriptive advantage** – the free-ranging eye of a third-person narrator can pick out 'telling details' freely and unselfconsciously, particularly helpful when writing set-up □

Now take your responses to both questions and distil each of your ten answers into a single word or phrase:

_____

_____

_____

_____

_____

_____

_____

_____

_____

_____

_____

_____

_____

_____

_____

_____

_____

_____

_____

The beginnings of your quiver of writing strategies are blueprinted above. Consider it a bullet list you can exploit in your writing when you consider the fundamental question of the narrator. Let's look at how you can move on to make more narrative choices that maximize your strengths and values as a writer.

→ Types of narrator: Centre-stage, without starring

The narrator defines and controls how a reader experiences a creative piece. Sometimes the narrator is an actual character in the story, sometimes they're the 'authorial consciousness' we feel in a poem or description of a landscape, or in an *auteur*-style movie.

In biography and life writing, as in much non-fiction, the narrator may never step forward on the page, and make a statement or advance an opinion – but they exist throughout the text as an entity whose diction, worldview and other authorial choices direct how we apprehend their subject. These choices include:

▶ What the narrator includes, and what they leave out

▶ What they foreground, and what they efface

▶ What they give page space to and how

▶ When they reveal important information.

These choices make even an 'effaced', invisible narrator into a fully fleshed character in our minds as we read. When people talk about wanting to buy a favourite writer a drink, it's this interesting character of whom they're thinking.

→ Case study: The narrator's voice

David Niven's *The Moon's a Balloon* is a market-making book that won millions of readers as a global bestseller, and helped create the sector in which Stephen Fry and Bill Bryson excel.

Hollywood veteran Niven animated his bestselling memoir with a wry yet direct authorial voice. The effect, for millions of readers of *The Moon's a Balloon*, was as if they were experiencing Niven's charming and 'open-handed' manner directly.

Yet it begins with an uncomfortable shock:

> *Nessie, when I first saw her, was seventeen years old, honey-blonde, pretty rather than beautiful, the owner of a voluptuous but somehow innocent body and a pair of legs that went on for ever. She was a Piccadilly whore. I was a fourteen year-old heterosexual schoolboy, and I met her thanks to my stepfather.*
>
> (The Moon's a Balloon, 1994)

This is risky material. Published in 1971, not long after Penguin books had been prosecuted for selling *Lady Chatterley's Lover* (written half a century earlier by classic novelist D. H. Lawrence), such upfront sexual content in a book aimed at the mass market was a big risk to take.

To focus the nature of such sexual content, even in the so-called 'permissive society' of the time, on what promises to be intimacy between a barely teenage boy and a sex worker only a couple of years older, might be sailing too close to the wind for many. But, cheerfully to compound matters, the narrator does something almost unthinkable at this point. A parenthetical note, tacked on to the end of the short opening paragraph, reads:

> *If you would like to skip on and meet Nessie more fully, she reappears on page 41.*
>
> (The Moon's a Balloon, 1994)

Most jaws hit the floor here, I'd guess. Followed by many people fumbling ahead to page 41, no doubt, but finding a scene so witty and warmly written, so rich in humanity and devoid of prurience, that they turned back to the beginning to find out how these two interesting young people hooked up.

Exercise 12

FIRST IMPRESSIONS

What does Niven's opening do for you? Imagine that you know nothing except that Niven was a hugely respected star of Hollywood's golden years, and that this is his first book. What kind of reading experience does the first paragraph promise?

Write a few lines. Use words like 'prurient' or 'creepy' if that's what hit you first. But if you feel that, as a reader, you're being 'played two ways' by the author, explore that. Whatever Niven's opening paragraph makes you feel, try to break it down. Write down what triggered your dominant initial feeling, then make a bullet list of what else in these lines developed or affected that feeling:

_____

_____

_____

_____

_____

_____

_____

_____

_____

_____

_____

_____

_____

So what did you decide to focus on? It's quite tough, I think. For example, the language used to describe Nessie is more appreciative than is comfortable when the subject is a teenage sex worker. Niven is fondly remembering how Nessie first struck him when he was 14, and it's not easy to engage with an old man's fond tone when the subject is a teenage prostitute.

But the baldness of the revelation about Nessie's work – and the hint of Niven's own lot in life at the time – combines with the directness of the voice (particularly the challenge to skip ahead to the sex scene, if that's what you want to do) to undercut the feelings the first lines provoke, compellingly if unsettlingly.

The truth is, I think, that it's meant to be a tough opening. Niven is writing about something that happened when he was 14 'thanks to my stepfather'. The suggestion of abuse in both Niven's and Nessie's childhoods is strong, at a time when people didn't talk about child abuse. As the pages that follow the opening reveal, Niven's purpose here is to write about his own childhood abuse in this chapter, from an adult perspective.

Exercise 13

OPENING LINES AND NARRATIVE CHOICES

Niven was writing about child abuse in this 1972 publication, a subject generally hushed up at the time. What narrative strategies can you see Niven using in this opening paragraph (including its parenthetical note) to overcome the difficulties of discussing such issues, given the prevailing climate of silence?

_____

_____

_____

_____

_____

The answer is quite a few. A long, attention-grabbing first sentence is followed by a short punchy one. It's a classic hook line and punchline, to pique attention and reward it. The punchline second sentence is both a pay-off and a shocking development that unsettles us. A 17-year-old girl should not be a veteran of the inner-city sex trade. The appreciative language used to describe her at first glance makes uncomfortable reading.

But Niven's command of the narrative voice is so confident that he takes extraordinary risks, even as he fires off this dangerous opening gambit. He proceeds directly to making an unsettling joke about public prurience driving the celebrity biography market, by pulling a strong-register postmodern move in his parenthetical coda to the paragraph (when the first wave of postmodern novelists, like Vonnegut and Don DeLillo, were still young men).

Yet the material of this opening paragraph is still pretty rich for most people's blood, I'd guess. Most of us didn't pick up charming, talented David Niven's memoir hoping it would kick off with the promise of a sex scene between two young teenagers – one of whom is barely out of puberty, the other working as an inner-city prostitute yet just a couple of years older.

The appreciative language used to describe Nessie is in these terms uncomfortable. But Niven is writing about himself at 14, and as a growing lad – we are soon to discover – it turns out that he can be forgiven for appreciating an attractive girl.

Because Niven is telling his own, truthful story here, and Nessie is a ray of sunshine to his 14-year-old self. What comes before Nessie for the young Niven is painful, long-term childhood abuse. Whatever caused Nessie to be a three-year veteran of the game at 17 is something that the young Niven can connect with by the time they meet.

So, as we read up to the notorious page 41, we entirely forget that the young Niven is about to hook up with Nessie because what happens in the interim is a grim catalogue of abuse and ill-treatment that rivets our engagement. The boy Niven is bullied and alienated by his stepfather, sent to appalling schools where he is physically and sexually abused, and generally persecuted for his failings to 'fit the mould' and get onto the military career conveyor belt while still barely a boy.

The future star responds by becoming a scamp: the young Niven copes with tough circumstances by acting up as the class clown, but is forced to confine his larks after disastrous expulsions from increasingly last-ditch schools. By the age of 14 Niven has borne horrible conditions for much of his life and is greatly owed a human connection, we feel as readers. The delightful Nessie, herself escaping a tough past and finding autonomy in the only way available, provides one.

Exercise 14

OPENING CHOICES – MAXIMIZING OPTIONS

Look at Niven's opening paragraph again. Can you see subtle places where Niven is 'spinning' the strong-register content of his material? Look closely at the particular choices Niven's narrator makes, note them down, and jot in your thoughts and observations.

_____

_____

_____

_____

_____

_____

_____

_____

_____

_____

_____

_____

_____

_____

_____

_____

_____

_____

I think there are several interesting choices at work here. The language used to describe Nessie is physical, certainly, and shocking in the context of a teenage sex worker, and for a mass-market Hollywood star of the time. Certainly, its millions of readers didn't pick up the book expecting the first lines to venture into such territory.

But there are a few places here where the narrator's choices belie his serious intent, and begin to work toward it. Niven's story is of how two kids from abusive backgrounds built a positive and supportive relationship in their teens that lasted as long as it could – several years, it turns out.

The particular words used to describe Nessie are interesting:

▶ She's 'honey-blonde', not bottle-blonde or platinum. The narrator compares her blondeness to something nutritious and wholesome.
▶ She's 'pretty rather than beautiful', which, if the narrator had lecherous intent, wouldn't be the obvious choice. In exploitative, pornographic writing, clichéd markers of desirability are used to depersonalize female subjects, as if they're no more than arousing amalgamation of porcelain skin, lustrous tresses, full sensual lips, etc.

'Pretty' makes Nessie seem like a girl who has a pretty way about her; someone beautiful can be sulky and ill-tempered and still be beautiful. The narrator wants us to care about Nessie, to connect with her a little more than simply as a 'beauty'.

The description of her body and legs are certainly sexualising, but up to this point in the opening paragraph Niven could still be talking about a teenage sweetheart met at church. Despite the shock of the next line, revealing Nessie's profession, the narrator's choices in this paragraph function as careful, subtle set-up. Nessie may be working the streets for a living, as it turns out, but we can take what this paragraph says about her at face value: she's a fair young woman making the best of bad circumstances.

Exercise 15

RECASTING INITIAL IMPRESSIONS

How has your perspective on Niven's first paragraph changed over the course of this exercise? Look at your answers to the questions so far, and list the steps you took in your thinking between them.

_____

_____

_____

_____

_____

_____

_____

_____

_____

_____

_____

_____

_____

_____

_____

_____

_____

_____

Well done if you were able to break down some of the processes you went through as you thought about the way this short, punchy paragraph of Niven's is put together.

It's a strong-register piece of writing: a bold hook designed both to grab a reader's attention and prepare them for a positive story of childhood abuse, focusing on the mutual support two survivors gave each other in their teens. Niven took some big risks with his narrator, not to mention his public image, to begin his long-awaited memoir by showing an abused childhood and the unorthodox ways he escaped it.

So, the notorious page 41 is indeed the beginning of a sex scene between the abused underage Niven and a barely older sex worker. It's a tender scene leavened by Nessie's warmth and wit, and the two form a close friendship that is only interrupted by war. Their story is of two survivors helping each other find their feet after crippling childhoods – at least, as much as two teenagers can.

Niven's opening paragraph therefore sets up a powerful story of surviving adversity in childhood, which pays off in a hugely positive way. The story of Niven and Nessie is a delight to read, full of good-hearted saucy wit and positive human experiences for the pair. But it's also a master class – in its single-paragraph set-up to a story of abuse in childhood – in making choices about your narrator that serve your piece from its opening lines. Niven's opening boldness and risk-taking grab a reader's attention, and hold it through a tough story about surviving a harsh childhood.

→ Types of narrator: The 'background', or effaced, narrator

An effaced narrator stays in the background, but is present throughout the piece as an organizing consciousness who presents and mediates the material. Effaced narrators are especially useful in poetry, where the author wants to let the subject 'speak for itself' without putting a figure in the landscape to observe it.

In storytelling writing, effaced narrators are used to give the illusion of detached access, as if one wall of a room has been peeled away so a reader can see the people inside – hear what they're saying, watch what they're doing, and make judgements from how they accomplish both.

This is called fourth-wall realism and it's the standard narrative mode of most creative writing. As the name implies, it's a technique that's all about letting the reader experience the piece as closely as possible while maintaining enough distance to see the big picture.

But fourth-wall realism isn't a matter of letting the reader sit back and watch things unfold, as if they were watching a movie. The fourth-wall effect can be combined with different narrative positions to achieve different effects. It's a matter of horses for courses: let's explore how authors maximize these choices.

BACKGROUND VERSUS FOREGROUND NARRATOR

David Niven's memoir necessarily uses a foregrounded, first-person narrator to tell the story of his life. Fiction often uses an effaced, third-person narrator so that there's nothing 'in the way' of the story for a reader. But often, when an author wants to achieve powerful effects, a background narrator can be moved dramatically to the foreground.

Charles Dickens was a great social critic as well as a great storyteller, identifying injustices and abuses and doing his utmost to make a reader care passionately about them. To achieve this, he often combined fourth-wall access with a foregrounded narrator, for several reasons.

First, stories of social criticism tend to be on the grim side, so a foregrounded narrator can step forward and make jokes, leavening dour realities with much-needed humour. In Dickens's greatest and last completed novel, *Our Mutual Friend*, the snouts-in-the-trough wealthy of the story are joyfully mocked as they're introduced at a fancy dinner. The narrator is a beard-tweaking jester in this scene, flitting merrily about the table to report on the unfolding absurdities.

The narrator's own energy foregrounds him here, as his relentless mockeries dissolve the fourth-wall perspective and make us feel as if we're flitting around the table too. A more straightforward background-to-foreground shift that Dickens used often was to have the narrator step forward on the page, to propose real-world solutions to problems discussed in the story. The pigs-in-clover wealthy controlled provision for the poor in Dickens's time, and the narrator of *Our Mutual Friend* steps forward to make savagely satirical direct appeals to the 'Lords, Ladies, and Honourable Boards' who preside over the fate of the most vulnerable.

Dickens used foregrounding as an extreme tactic in his social criticism project, but other classic authors used techniques of foregrounding for plain storytelling purposes. Charlotte Brontë famously had a narrator speak from the foreground directly 'into the camera', in order to mediate a love story's foregone conclusion: 'Reader, I married him.'

Other great novelists have deployed an entirely effaced, 'invisible' narrator in order to power the effects of their seminal works: George Orwell combined fourth-wall access with an effaced narrator, so that the special worlds and characters of novels like *Animal Farm* and *Nineteen Eighty-Four* could be realized for the reader directly and viscerally.

FOREGROUNDING A NARRATOR

Think of someone you really don't like. Someone who gets your goat, rustles your jimmies, and gives you the pip. It could be someone at work, it could be a celebrity, or even a boorish relative: someone who unfailingly annoys you.

Now write two short paragraphs that are a neutral presentation of this individual. Don't include information of which you have special knowledge, such as the reason you don't like this person; use only the facts which are commonly known. Write it in the third person, with the narrator in the background: for example, *Rudolf De Ked is manager at De Ked Enterprises, boss of a dozen De Ked personnel including me.*

_____

_____

_____

_____

_____

_____

_____

Neutral in its every point? Narrator nicely in the background? Then you've earned part two of this exercise. Keep the same facts, but foreground the narrator, and let rip. Demolish this dolt. Remember, there's no 'I' here – keep it in the third person. And if you get stuck, go back and change your initial choices to ones that have more potential for 'spinning' into a negative light now. Gloves off!

_____

_____

_____

_____

_____

_____

_____

_____

_____

_____

_____

_____

_____

_____

_____

_____

_____

_____

_____

As I hope you've found out to your satisfaction, narrative position can make a big difference. Moving into the foreground closes the distance between a third-person narrative voice and reader, allowing all kinds of partiality and 'spin' to be applied.

→ Types of narrator: First-person narrators

A first-person narrator is right up there on the page. In poetry, they signal their presence with the initial pronoun choices:

> *That's my last Duchess painted on the wall*
>
> Robert Browning, 'My Last Duchess'
>
> *Whose woods these are I think I know*
>
> Robert Frost, 'Stopping by Woods on a Snowy Evening'

In fiction, the narrator stepping forward and introducing themself at the start of a piece is a convention so established that many great writers choose to surprise readers by playing with the idea of an introduction:

▶ In *Moby Dick*, Herman Melville transcends the distance between a narrator made of ink and paper and a reader by opening with a proffered hand: 'Call me Ishmael.'

▶ *The Catcher in the Rye* begins with the narrator refusing to introduce himself in the usual way – 'all that David Copperfield kind of crap' – because he wants the reader to judge him by what he thinks and does, rather than by his privileged upbringing. This character's refusal to introduce himself is, of course, the perfect introduction for this character.

A first-person narrator can hit the ground running, inducting us quickly into a story with a compelling authorial voice. It needn't be a confident first-person voice, but the perspectives and possibilities of the first person permit a creative author to get straight into the telling.

Where to next?

Whether first person or third, background or right up in the story, the choice of narrator in a creative piece is crucial. Constructing the narrative position to fit the story is a choice-making process for creative writers seeking to maximize the readability of their material.

In the next chapter we'll start putting our narrators to work, as we explore the principle technique of creative writing. From line-by-line writing to the overarching structure of a piece, we'll discover how creative authors use one golden rule to bring their writing to life on the page.

Ideas and inspirations

▶ The obvious narrator for a creative piece is not always the optimal choice. Making optimal narrative choices gets creative pieces cooking on the page.

▶ The narrator acts as liaison between reader and author, but they can equally enhance or obscure the true picture.

▶ Your reading and enjoyment of on-screen stories have already taught you a lot about narrative strategies that authors deploy to maximize the impact of their work. You already possess a valuable knowledge base of narrative techniques in action.

▶ Constructing a narrator to fit each creative piece maximizes opportunities to flex your creative potential.

4 The first rule of creative writing

In this chapter you will learn:

- About the crucial difference between 'telling' and 'showing' in creative writing.
- About the first rule of creative writing, and how to use it to make your work come alive on the page.
- How the Show Don't Tell technique generates reader engagement, and permits powerful progression in a piece – even using nothing but nuance.

→ The golden rule

Show Don't Tell is the primary rule of creative writing. It means what it says: *show* your reader things, don't *tell* them about them.

Writing that 'tells', instead of showing, is not creative writing – it's a report. 'Showing' is what makes writing creative.

The reasons for this repay exploration. Telling forces a reader into a passive position, where they're simply receiving information. Showing invites them to engage with a piece, as they interpret what they see, infer from it, and project what they've concluded forward into the unfolding action.

Telling means handing down information to your reader, like a lazy schoolteacher. Showing means inviting them to participate in your story. Want to know a sure-fire way to lose an agent's or editor's interest immediately? Open your creative piece with the main character reflecting:

Sebastian gazed out of the time-worn mullioned window as the shadows lengthened. It had been on just such a summer's eve that he'd arrived at Tremblynge Towers as a fresh-faced heir to the dukedom; now the shadows in his ravaged jaw deepened even as they encroached across the weed-tangled croquet lawn. Motes of dust illuminated by rays of setting sunlight danced like reproachful faeries around his head, as if to whisper If only you'd laid off the sauce and the gee-gees, old lad…*

This is, of course, telling, not showing. The converse might be something like:

The eleventh Duke of Trembly received news of the latest disaster at dusk, with his breakfast. He drank two fingers of room-temperature vodka, vomited, then refreshed himself direct from the bottle. His morning routine thus complete, he checked the racing results, and groaned; then, cradling the bottle like a cat, wove his way back to bed past portraits of his ancestors on the walls and puddles of rainwater on the rotting Persian carpet.

Showing rather than telling means using action. Even if a character is alone – *especially* if a character is alone – their actions can speak volumes. It's a matter of psychology, of the human condition: we show how we feel, and interpret what we see in others. Whatever kind of writer you are, your readers are hardwired to pick up on nuance in human behaviour: your job is to make it meaningful.

→ Case study: Showing, not telling, with nuance

'Bahnhofstrasse' is a beautiful, complex yet extremely short poem written by James Joyce whilst teaching English in Switzerland, in order to fund his writing. It's a moving lament in two short stanzas, spoken by a man feeling the passage of time. The first runs:

> *The eyes that mock me sign the way*
> *Whereto I pass at eve of day.*
> *Grey way, whose violet signals are*
> *The trysting and the twining star.*
>
> (Poems and Shorter Writings, 2001)

This short but lilting opening verse makes me picture a tired-looking guy plodding home from his commute at dusk, as the streetlamps flicker on in the side-streets around the railway station, and the working girls take up their positions in doorways.

This intense first stanza introduces a lot of information, in just four lines – yet it also progresses the narrator from an opening position to a developed position. He begins by feeling mocked by the derisive eyes of the prostitutes, who know he can't afford them – literally, or because he doesn't want to lose such stability as he has in life. The tension between the speaker's provoked sexuality and his self-control is perhaps expressed in the slight bitterness of 'eyes that mock', but the speaker ends the verse with a beautiful line, which perhaps recalls his own youthful 'trysting'.

The speaker has moved from being made uncomfortable by the brazen sexuality of the working girls in the streets, to translating his arousal into intense sensual memory: 'trysting' can be read literally here, but 'twining' is used for its sound, rhythm and onomatopoeic associations – an unexpected word that involves us sensually in its sound. Joyce engineers an exquisite poetic pay-off to the rapid progression of narrative position in this opening stanza.

The second stanza keeps up the pace:

> *Ah star of evil! Star of pain!*
> *High-hearted youth comes not again*
> *Nor old heart's wisdom yet to know*
> *The signs that mock me as I go.*
>
> (Poems and Shorter Writings, 2001)

The speaker, in the midst of his 'grey way', is moved to soul-deep exclamation, followed by a longing for the peace of maturity – a time, certainly, when youth and the pain of losing it will be less fresh. Despite the utmost brevity, Joyce's poem achieves powerful engagement with some of the thorniest inner struggles of human existence. Every carefully chosen word shows us a new facet on the speaker's soul and its processing of its condition and fate, creating a beautifully focused and moving piece.

SHOW DON'T TELL AND NUANCE

Write a few short paragraphs on the following scenario:

Someone is absorbed in an activity – on a laptop in a city coffee shop; chopping wood in the wilderness – but they are harbouring a secret. Not brooding about it, not pondering it, just harbouring it. Someone unrelated to the secret enters the frame and engages them, and suddenly the secret is in danger of spilling out.

Work on keeping it short and punchy, and close the scene if you can.

_____

_____

_____

_____

_____

_____

_____

_____

_____

_____

_____

_____

_____

_____

_____

_____

_____

_____

_____

Did you use nuanced action to show about the secret? Body language, perhaps, to show that a secret was being harboured? Or were the simmering emotions in your scene rattling the lid on the pan? Perhaps what the second person brought into the room triggered the first. How did you set up the triggering? And did you manage to follow through from it?

There are many ways to play this scene, all good. It's a very human position, to hold something inside while trying not to show it, and perhaps a necessary part of life. So there's a wide variety of both nuanced and upfront human behaviours to choose from, for a writer seeking to bring this scenario to life. Its inner life translates naturally into physical action, as is true of most 'charged' human encounters – a social species is necessarily one whose members are skilled at not rocking the boat. The human capacity to hide things is boundless; a narrator who can show a reader the depth below the surface is a narrator who can engage with the big issues of life.

→ Show Don't Tell analysis: Opening lines of classic works

LONGITUDE BY DAVA SOBEL

The runaway success of this biography revitalized the non-fiction market, almost overnight. Its story focuses on mathematics and geometry – not subjects that the mass market frequently clamours for – but Sobel gets her readers into her tale and turning pages by opening thus:

> *Once on a Wednesday excursion when I was a little girl, my father bought me a beaded wire ball which I loved. At a touch, I could collapse the toy into a flat coil between my palms, or pop it open to make a hollow sphere.*

These wire-balls were common items in the 1970s and 1980s, sold as pocket-money toys. Sobel's choice is a democratic one – most of her readers would remember these things – and extremely canny. Because she needs to explain to a general reader what latitude and longitude are, she gives us a feel-good visual image upfront – a familiar wire-ball toy – to hold in our heads, and refer back to when the necessary complexity comes.

'Telling' would have been the standard way to start a book of this nature, listing the date and birthplace of the biography's subject. But this 'showing' approach, with its everyday diction and feel-good focus, enabled Sobel to make a difficult concept visually accessible from the start, and helped her modest historical biography become a runaway bestseller.

LORD OF THE FLIES BY WILLIAM GOLDING

This classic novel is renowned for its gripping story and the insights it provokes. Here's how it opens:

> *The boy with fair hair lowered himself down the last few feet of rock and began to pick his way toward the lagoon. Though he had taken off his school sweater and trailed it now from one hand, his grey shirt stuck to him and his hair was plastered to his forehead.*

We're shown a schoolboy, scrambling over seaside rocks. We're pretty sure we know what's going on in this story, as we read these opening lines. This is some sort of school trip, where one boy has wandered off from the rest.

Our assumption couldn't be further from the mark: this boy is scrambling over seaside rocks because a plane full of school kids has just crashed on a desert island, killing all the adults. I once taught a class to advanced writing students where I presented this scenario, lightly disguised: all but one opted to start with the plane crash, not with the boy scrambling over rocks in its aftermath. The student who chose the same opening as Golding was the only one who scored a publishing deal afterward.

The plane crash, which Golding and my star student chose to put in the backstory, is in many ways an attractive opening for a writer seeking to grip and entertain a reader. It's replete with opportunities for tense, compelling action – first, one engine starts to sputter, and the pilot takes evasive action, before problems compound (a sudden squall, for example) and the plane enters its terminal dive. Imagine the horror of the passengers, as the crashing realization hits, that reality as they know it is now just a memory. A plane-crash scene would be a breezy everyday situation degrading to tense, escalating action, horror and mortal fear – what more could an author hope for, to get a reader turning pages eagerly?

But the action of the novel, and its big question, is how the boys can survive without adults, shelter or supplies. Starting the novel with the plane crash would force this terrible question into the tail end of an incident, not foreground it from the opening lines. By beginning his first scene after the plane crash, Golding drives home the full horror of the situation that is the engine of his renowned story.

'MY LAST DUCHESS' BY ROBERT BROWNING

Famed for its dramatic intensity, Browning's poem opens by literally 'showing':

> *That's my last Duchess painted on the wall,*
> *Looking as if she were alive. I call*
> *That piece a wonder, now: Frà Pandolf's hands*
> *Worked busily a day and there she stands.*
> *Will't please you sit and look at her?*

The speaker is a Renaissance duke entertaining a guest. His opening lines are a courtly invitation to enjoy the work of a famous artist whom he commissioned. The Duke sounds almost subservient in his courteousness to his guest: 'Will't please you…'

But, as the poem develops, we realize that this courtliness is a mask. The Duke coolly explains how his last Duchess managed to displease him, by failing to remain sufficiently aloof from all but her noble husband:

> *[…] She had*
> *A heart – how shall I say? – too soon made glad*

For evidence he cites a stroll in the palace orchard, when she smiled because someone picked cherry blossoms for her.

With mounting horror, we realize that this Duchess's human warmth was, for the Duke, a fatal flaw. He 'gave commands | Then all smiles stopped'. As the poem concludes, we realize that the Duke is giving a barely veiled warning to the wealthy parents of his next bride. In showing us the horrible truth about what happened to the last Duchess, Browning delivers everything we need to know about the Duke, and the imperatives of a patriarchal privileged class.

⏰ Exercise 18

USING SHOW DON'T TELL TO OPEN PIECES

What's your best story about a Christmas mishap? Even if you don't do Christmas, everyone who lives in a country that grinds to a halt for a week has one: the plumbing or roofing emergency; the workplace or neighbourhood party; the sudden reappearance of prodigal miscreants; the fallen tree blocking escape from a disagreeable relative's village.

Write your story out as a scene using actions alone to tell your reader what they need to know. The only way to encode information in your scene is in what your characters do and say.

_____

_____

_____

_____

_____

_____

_____

_____

_____

_____

_____

_____

_____

→ Showing not telling: A practical guide

The big leap all budding writers make is when they move from mainly telling in their writing to mainly showing. Suddenly their writing shifts into gear: it may still feel like squeezing blood from a stone, but on the page it's starting to cook.

As with all great leaps forward in personal development, it's mostly a result of practice, and of getting into the right headspace. The first step toward the latter is to see the world like a writer, and that means seeing it differently.

You're already well adept at seeing things differently as you move through life. As a young child, you probably loved the rain. Rain was a wonderful thing that made everything lustrous and lucid, providing fascinating drops on windows to 'race' against their fellows, and puddles to splash in when the downpour was past.

Now rain is what makes your commute to work a misery, wrecks your weekend plans: it's a drag. So look at the rain differently, and try to see it as you've seen it before; the following practical exercise should help you make the mental sidestep from your adult, distracted way of experiencing what's around you, to how you perceived the world when it was all still new.

 *Exercise 19*

RECALIBRATING YOUR CREATIVE EYE

Check the weather forecast every day and when rain is coming, watch out for the signs. Feel the change in the air, and the wind, and look for mackerel-sky cloud or the ragged grey bottoms of towering thunderheads. If there's rain forecast for the weekend, and you can free up some time, then get up somewhere high as the weather's moving in, and appreciate what it does to the light, before and after and during the rainfall.

When it's beginning to pass over (tip: wait till you can hear individual drips from gutters, and birds beginning to chatter), don your rain boots and get out there. Smell public parks after rain, tight-knit terraced streets, leafy suburban avenues, and windswept concrete precincts. Record what your senses pick up on your phone or in a notebook – write them up later and file them under 'Scene-setting Details'. Watch what the birds do during the deluge and how they perk up toward its end. Become a connoisseur of cumulostratus, of thunderhead and ground fog, of drizzle and mizzle and downpour. Finally, splash in a few puddles (tip: do not attempt this around urban gang members or riot police, few of whom are in touch with their inner child).

Soon you'll come to see the rain as you first saw it: as special, as a wonderful deviation from the everyday, something that makes colours deeper and light lucent. You'll remember the turning points on your journey – those moments when you realized that what you were experiencing out in the weather was pretty special – and the dedication and thought processes that helped you make this turnaround in your perceptions, and begin to apply them to other things you see and experience. Shifting from the everyday to your writerly way of seeing will become like a change of mental gait as you stride into the world, senses sharpened and ready for experience.

→ Show Don't Tell: Freshening the everyday

While you're waiting for rain, take a look at this. It's from a wonderful poem by Craig Raine, whose title explains it all: 'A Martian Sends a Postcard Home'. Can you guess what's being described here?

> *In homes a haunted apparatus sleeps,*
> *that snores when you pick it up.*
> *If the ghost cries they carry it*
> *to their lips and soothe it to sleep*
> *with sounds. And yet they wake it up*
> *deliberately by tickling it with a finger.*

The answer is, of course a landline phone (note to younger readers: the analogue dial tone was a low mechanical purr). Raine's poetic transmutation makes interesting points about our relationship with technology by showing us an everyday object in a new way – a telephone as a demanding but somnolent ghost.

The poem is full of everyday things presented in a new light: books are 'birds with many wings', which sometimes 'perch on the hand', causing the 'eyes to melt | Or the 'body to shriek with pain'. Mist is 'when the sky is tired of flight', rain is 'when the earth is television'. The author takes a step sideways from the world to report on its phenomena in a fresh and revelatory way.

Exercise 20

A MARTIAN POSTCARD

Write your own extraterrestrial postcard home. Schedule three trips out into the world with your notebook – one first thing in the morning, one at a busy noontime, one on a quiet evening – and concentrate on seeing things in a different way. On your morning trip, for example, you might pick up on the contemporary phenomena of people buying scratch cards, or walking reverently behind dogs, bearing their excrement. First, make the familiar strange, then see if you can find meaning in the strangeness – for example, the morning rituals of scratch cards and poop bags could suggest religious devotions to your Martian.

_____

_____

_____

_____

_____

_____

_____

_____

_____

_____

_____

_____

Where to next?

 Seeing the world differently – like a writer sees it – isn't just something that makes writers interesting people. Collecting insightful perspectives on the world is a creative author's stock-in-trade, as they translate what they see into meaningful insight on the page.

The ability to show, rather than tell, becomes crucial to writers seeking to create characters that come alive on the page, and show us great truths about humanity in how they respond to events – and sometimes drive them.

In the next chapter we'll explore in detail the key techniques of creating credible and compelling characters, with the vigour to 'arc' through the action of a creative piece and capture reader's emotions and imaginations.

Ideas and inspirations

▶ The Show Don't Tell technique empowers authors to involve readers in their work from the opening lines onward.

▶ Making Show Don't Tell your line-by-line credo will open up options to turn opening situations into intriguing developments in your writing.

▶ Learning to see the everyday with depth and dimensionality is a skill that can be practised wherever you need to be from day to day.

▶ Exploring the multiple perspectives writers train themselves to see in the everyday will generate striking and original thought processes as you write.

5 Creating characters and action

→ Creating living characters

Following the principle of Show Don't Tell makes the narrator of a creative piece someone we want to listen to. With their intriguing, writerly ways of seeing things differently, creative authors use fresh perspectives on the page to invite a reader's participation in their writing, making the human 'voices' of their pieces vivid and interesting to read. Good narrators are people we want to spend time with, because of their power to show us new perspectives on the panorama of life.

The other human presences on the creative page are, of course, characters. From great romantic heroines to chilling serial killers, from hard-bitten life writing to narrative poetry, three-dimensional characters make creative pieces vivid, moving and meaningful.

Exercise 21

CHARACTERIZATION AND CHARACTER DEVELOPMENT

Choose a favourite character from a book you've enjoyed. How does this character seem to the world when they first appear in the book? List five things about how they 'come across' when you first meet them on the page.

_____

_____

_____

_____

_____

_____

_____

_____

_____

_____

_____

_____

_____

_____

Now use hindsight. What are the hidden depths that make this character so engaging to follow? Again, list five qualities if you can.

Can you trace lines between your second set of answers and your first? Chances are that you can. Authors build characters so that a narrative's events can develop them, revealing new facets and hidden depths, which is what makes our favourite characters so memorable. In this chapter we'll explore how writers breathe life into characters and practise the key tried-and-tested techniques.

→ 'Coming alive' on the page

A creative author breathes life into characters. When this fails to happen, we call the results 'wooden' or 'two-dimensional'. Characters who don't come alive on the page make for an effortful read at best, yet I've lost count of how many manuscripts I've read with intriguing plotting and interesting ideas but characters flat as pancakes.

Much of the problem derives from 'drawing from life'. Budding authors are encouraged to 'write what you know', and for many that means the *people* they know. They fix on a certain kind of person for their piece, and cherry-pick traits from other people they've encountered in life to 'flesh out' the character.

A sure sign of this approach is when the character is presented as if the author is trying to match-make, piling up engaging quirks along with every nugget of potential interest from the 'backstory'. Hence, in the crime-fiction field, for example, the slush-pile is overflowing with detectives who grew up on the mean streets but now divide their time between cooking cordon bleu in their state-of-the-art kitchen and skydiving while playing Dixieland sax.

The writerly approach to creating characters that live and breathe on the page is a lot simpler. Rather than trying to pick up on cultural clues to create someone attractive enough to want to read about, we use the principle of Show Don't Tell – as explored in the last chapter – to give depth and dimension to the characters that populate our pages.

 *Exercise 22*

THE SHOW DON'T TELL PRINCIPLE IN CHARACTER CREATION

Think of a playboy Brit tough-guy who likes his refreshments shaken not stirred. I'll wager you can even say 'shaken not stirred' with the key actor's accent if you try (extra points if you sign off with 'shweetheart').

Ian Fleming's extraordinary creation, 007, is one of the longest-lived characters in popular culture. The first Bond novels were published in the 1950s; the movies are still going strong. Their hero's catchphrases are globally recognized, and have been for half a century. There's a particular reason for that, and it's not the movies' awful puns.

James Bond is a classy kind of guy, equally suave at the helm of a speedboat, at the baccarat table, or in the boudoir. His alter ego, 007, is a ruthless, highly trained, government-licensed killer.

But there's no Jekyll and Hyde going on here. They're different sides of the same guy, and the real thrills in the Bond tales – reliably impeccable chase scenes aside – is when both kick in at once. When the handsome lounge lizard who's been charming the duplicitous beauty all evening smoothly suggests she drop the act then produces a semi-automatic to assist her decision-making, for example. Or when Bond and a big cheese move from verbal power-plays to all-out battle.

James Bond is an endlessly tractable character because of this contrast between surface and depth. On the outside he's an attractive guy who out-suaves rivals and waltzes women into bed. Behind the façade he's a lethal, expert assassin. When both sides of this character are shown (particularly when the two combine – James Bond in full effect), the consequences set pulses racing, again and again.

 So let's try working with surface and depth right now. List five attractive qualities you possess. Focus on those that don't get sufficient recognition in life, for the most part.

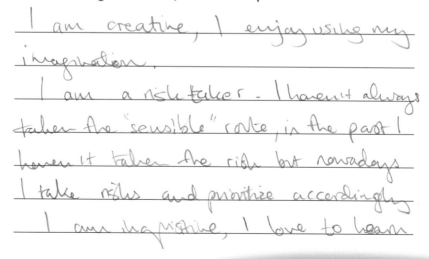

I am creative, I enjoy using my imagination,
I am a risk taker - I haven't always taken the "sensible" route, in the past I haven't taken the risk but nowadays I take risks and prioritize accordingly
I am inquisitive, I love to learn

about the mysteries of life [the universe + everything].

When truly engaged with my SELF, I put 100% effort into what I do. Dedicated

I feel on the edge of society, something ~~caused~~ by my life's circumstances + the choices I've made. These days I don't go along with typical rythums of society, can you call that Independant minded?

Stuck? Try a few of these: You're inquisitive, because you're trying this exercise. You're tenacious, because you're into the fifth chapter here. You're creative, because you're trying your hand at creative writing. You've an appetite for new experiences, or you wouldn't be reading this book at all – try 'adventurous' as your keyword.

Now think of a character from your own writing, and how you've imagined them so far. If you wanted to show your reader that this character has each of the qualities you've listed above, how would you do it? Try sketching at least a couple of ways for each of your five qualities.

Pit: creative - the animal camp.
          - he could solve a prob ingeniously

Risktaking - offering to save freya without a thought
          - he could do something heroic

Inquisitive - he could ask alot of questions
          - he could get into trouble due to him having to take a look / interrogate

Dedicated - show that he doesn't give up ie. looking for freya, helping Edric.
          - spends / invests alot of time into carving?

I hope you found that working with qualities you possess yourself
was a help in that exercise. Abstract 'qualities' can sometimes
be thorny to translate into meaningful action, but you know from
experience how the qualities you listed sometimes find expression
in everyday life. Tracing believably human interconnections between
surface and depth, in response to the events of a narrative, is the key
to successful character creation.

→ Characterization and deep character

Characters that live and breathe on the page are fluid. Whether we're
writing biography, fiction, drama or poetry, we're not writing about
static people – definable only by their status, possessions and quirky
hobbies – but about individuals undergoing meaningful change:

▶ The central character of Thomas Hardy's poem 'The Darkling
Thrush', like that of Robert Frost's 'Stopping by Woods on a Snowy
Evening', moves from isolation and fatalistic despair at the start of
the poem to reconnecting with the world at its end.

▶ The heroine of I Know Why the Caged Bird Sings moves from being
a little girl stuttering over her lines in church, to spending years as a
shell-shocked child rape victim, to becoming a woman rebuilding her
connection to life.

Characters in creative writing move from opening positions – their
characterization, their place in life at the start of the piece – to closing
positions that resolve and make meaningful what's gone before. We
call this process **character development**. When there is a coherent
progression of character development, in response to the events of a
creative piece, we call the 'map' of the progression a **character arc**.

→ Character development and character arcs

The heroine of *The Bell Jar* is 'living the dream' at the start of Sylvia Plath's remarkable piece of life writing. She's won a glittering summer interning at a top magazine in New York, all expenses paid, and with a first-class ticket to the A-list life that is hers for the taking.

By the end of the book she's living in a mental hospital, with terrible experiences behind her, yet is receiving helpful treatment at last and is responding. The heroine arcs from success that's tainted by mental illness, to 'failure' (in material terms) bolstered by self-understanding.

The characterization of the speaker in Hardy's 'The Darkling Thrush' is of a man isolated from his fellows, perhaps foolishly on such a bitter winter afternoon. But in its telling the poem reveals his deep character: that of a man pausing in life to consider the bigger picture.

The poem's action – an elderly thrush singing, despite the midwinter lockdown – moves the speaker from an opening position of isolation and despair to a realization that, beyond his gloomy outlook, life is chugging along cheerfully, even in the frozen depth of winter. Character development is used to confirm life and humanity, as the speaker arcs from isolation and fatalism, in the fading of a freezing winter's day, to kindling a glimmer of hope.

But the same arc that produces an ambivalent or feel-good ending can also end in overwhelming negativity. In Orwell's *Nineteen Eighty-Four*, the hero begins with a powerful determination to be true to his inner self, and finds some success, yet ends a broken husk of a man. Character arcs, like the human processes they represent, are as diverse as humanity itself.

Exercise 23

BUILDING CHARACTER ARCS – OPENING POSITIONS

Try to trace lines between the following four opening positions on a character arc, and the four 'developed' positions beneath. The first row below represents four places where a character could be in life at the start of a creative piece; the second row represents where they are a third of the way through the piece.

LOYALTY   JUSTICE   COURAGE   SUCCESS

FAILURE   UNFAIRNESS   SPLIT ALLEGIANCE   FEAR

Find some interesting connections? Some thought-provoking developments of the opening value? Let's take it to the next level.

⏰ *Exercise 24*

CHARACTER ARCS – DEVELOPMENT AND PROGRESSION

Now try to connect the developed positions identified to where this character arc could be by the time it's two-thirds of the way through the piece. What's the next logical progression? Again, try to draw lines from the value positions in the top row down to the value positions beneath.

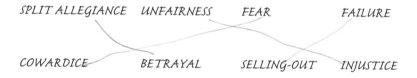

SPLIT ALLEGIANCE   UNFAIRNESS   FEAR   FAILURE

COWARDICE   BETRAYAL   SELLING-OUT   INJUSTICE

Getting interesting? I hope you've found for yourself how considering the idea of a character living in a state of justice or success, with everything peachy, can fruitfully be developed by the events of a narrative to living in a state of unfairness or of failure. These developed positions could then be progressed further, as the missteps taken already become a headlong stumble down slippery slopes: unfairness escalates to injustice, failure to selling-out.

Similarly, a character defined by their loyalty at the start of a piece can find their allegiances split, leading to a second developed position of betrayal. A character defined by their courage could come to know true fear, and have their courage collapse: now avoidance of life's troubles, cowardice, is what defines them.

Now let's take it to the end of the line.

Exercise 25

THE END OF THE LINE – CREATING MEANINGFUL RESOLUTIONS

What's a possible closing position on each of these character arcs? Try to figure it out logically based on the progression so far. If you're stuck, remember that these are very human progressions, so use your knowledge of our species here. Where will the first three of these two character arcs finish, if the character can't climb out of this particular hole? Can the character in the fourth arc find an easier way to live?

LOYALTY	COURAGE	JUSTICE	SUCCESS
SPLIT ALLEGIANCE	FEAR	UNFAIRNESS	FAILURE
BETRAYAL	COWARDICE	INJUSTICE	SELLING-OUT
? Guilt regret	?Blame on others	? revenge	? lack of integrity

This is a tough exercise, and your answers may depend as much on your perspective on the human condition as on your logical powers of reasoning.

The first three arcs, with their variables progressing in this order, result in 'down' endings – the character is forced to the very end of the line. For my money, the first three arcs play out like this:

LOYALTY	JUSTICE	COURAGE
SPLIT ALLEGIANCE	UNFAIRNESS	FEAR
BETRAYAL	INJUSTICE	COWARDICE
SELF-BETRAYAL	TYRANNY	COWARDICE PRETENDING TO BE COURAGE

Self-betrayal is an obvious end-of-the-line position. Living not with injustice but with tyranny is similarly so. Cowardice going under the guise of courage has proved a tractable end of the line in many tales of battlefield slaughter, especially World War I stories – but also in non-fiction bestsellers, such as memoirs focused on illness, or of wildest-dreams success and its attendant stresses.

→ 'Negative' arcs and redemption

Negative end-of-the-line positions don't mean negative endings to narratives. Tyranny is the natural end-of-the-line position in a memoir of escaping domestic abuse. The unbearable conditions at the end of the line spur change, and can even generate hope.

So stories that move from bad to worse to calamity are as much the stuff of last-ditch redemption stories as they are Faustian falls from grace. Big climaxes can be projected either way, as the character hits rock bottom, the very end of the line, and is spurred to go all out in the final furlong for good or ill.

But the fourth character arc we just worked with, starting from a position of material success, can end with spiritual success:

SUCCESS   *FAILURE*   *SELLING-OUT*   *GETTING BY*

'Getting by' is the true positive position on this arc. Material success is a matter of privilege for some and hard work for others. It's usually 'charged' negative in creative writing because it's the truth. Privileged people may dine at the top table and jet round the world, but they're insulated from real life – with all its beauty and grindstones, heartaches and treasured joys – by a bubble of luxury. 'Getting by' is true wealth: living within your means, being a part of the general effort. It's how people used to respond when asked how they were, before 'fine' erased the nuance and devalued the question.

→ Building character arcs from scratch

A writer looking to put human truths on the page can find the process dizzying at first. As soon as one lifts the lid on the human psyche, a tsunami of potential emotions and behaviours floods out. Trying to pick just a few to make a coherent progression can be like trying to find four-leaf clovers in a springtime pasture.

There can seem a bewildering array of choices, to a developing writer, in the range of human behaviours and motivations that could conceivably be put to use in a chosen scenario. Fortunately, writers have worked away at this problem for centuries, and have left their findings for us to read. A way of thinking has thus been developed that considers human progressions in life, for good or ill, as positive or negative progressions on a core value.

We've practised the process in the last exercises, finding how an opening value can be developed through a meaningful progression along an arc, building momentum and power. As you worked through the exercise, you'll have found ideas for stories – for events that can bring about the powerful changes we were working with – zipping into your mind unbidden, if you were in the right headspace. (If not, sketch out the character arcs on a new piece of paper, spacing the four progressions from the top to the bottom of the page, and see if you can't jot down a few ideas for events that could trigger such changes.)

In all dramatic writing – be it fiction, biography and memoir, poetry, or plays and screenplays – it's the fruitful use of fecund core values and arcs that gives narratives their impetus and power. It's these qualities that we'll explore in the next exercise, as we construct, from scratch, character arcs that are capable of catching a reader's attention and sustaining it.

Exercise 26

CREATING CHARACTER ARCS USING CORE VALUES

What seems to go wrong for most budding writers in this area is this: they begin the process of 'creating character' by identifying something they want to write about, then straight away try putting a human face on this particular facet of life's pageant.

For example, an author decides to write about modern-day greed, and instantly starts creating a hedge-fund manager in a glass-and-steel office, or a digital-hippy entrepreneur pottering in his vineyard. Making someone up from scratch is fun, and it's easy to get carried away with it. By the time they're ready to start writing, their tale has shrunk from a universal parable to a very particular set of circumstances, shedding meaning and intrigue in the process.

But, if they'd stuck with their original idea – greed – and not hared after a human face to front it, a much simpler route to satisfying story can be followed. It's a tried-and-tested route and is the process most creative authors follow. By thinking of greed as part of a potential progression of human values – an arc – other highpoints on this arc begin to suggest themselves.

 So where does greed come from? Which natural human need gets twisted to become greed?

_____

_____

Well done if you answered 'hunger'. It's the basic animal need that, improperly indulged in our world of excess, degrades into greed.

Greed is negative, but hunger is a natural drive we all share. Hunger tells us when we need food. In our wider lives, 'hunger' drives us to achieve, and to establish ourselves in life. It drives us to find a mate, and raise children if we can. Hunger is a good thing in life, when there are healthy ways to satiate it. Feeling honest, growling hunger after a day's exertion in the fresh air is an actively pleasant sensation – as is feeling hunger for experience when you know you're finally ready.

Exercise 27

DEVELOPING THE OPENING POSITION

 If healthy hunger is the first step on the road that leads to greed, what places lie in between? Jot down a few ideas if you can, then try to boil them down to a few single words.

_____

_____

_____

_____

_____

_____

_____

_____

_____

_____

_____

_____

_____

_____

_____

You're working with complex writerly tools now, and with some success already: your answer to this question is a sketch of a few possible escalating positions on a character arc. In a narrative about greed – be it biography or fiction, drama or poetry – you've created the bare bones of both a plot and an arcing central character.

Your answer's terminology may differ from mine, but for ease of use let's identify the following as possible developments on an arc between healthy hunger and unhealthy greed:

▶ **Satiety: This is the feeling you get when you've eaten enough, when you're full. It's the healthy signal that people who are greedy have trained themselves to ignore – whether it's a question of food, money or power.**

▶ **Insatiability: Greed isn't as bad as it can get for a person. When you've made the descent into greed, deliberately breaking natural satiety mechanisms, the hell of insatiability lies beneath.**

You'll notice that the word root of 'satiety' and 'insatiability' is the same. They're closely connected human states. Overriding the healthy state, for the sake of gratification, drives a human being inexorably toward decline – a downward trajectory that only grows in momentum.

· ·

BUILDING PROGRESSIONS FOR CHARACTER ARCS

Can you put the four possible positions we've identified as available to a greed arc into order? Can you draw arrows to create a logical flow from one position to the next?

_____

_____

_____

_____

_____

_____

_____

_____

_____

_____

_____

_____

_____

There are two likely answers to this question – both of them true. One is the logical downward arc from hunger, to satiety, to greed, to insatiability. A classic progression, from King Midas and King Croesus to *Wall Street* and *American Psycho*.

But think of someone who starts in life with a position beyond satiety thrust upon them. The child of a rich man who can't stop accumulating, for example. Someone who has beautiful spaces to live in, wonderful holidays every few months, tuitions and expensive hobbies and luxuries of every kind as the only things in their life.

This person might be beyond satiety already, but their story could still generate an upward ending, in a classic riches-to-rags to inner-riches progression: greed, then insatiability, then a crashing intervention – leading to hunger, perhaps for the first time as the character tries to live only on what they need, perhaps even needing to struggle to get it. Satiety, experienced truly and healthily, would create a feel-good closing position for a story of growth and redemption.

→ Creating arcs with core-value progressions

Flow charts are excellent visual tools for writers – in plotting, in structuring, in pacing, they're an invaluable means of putting thoughts down onto a blank page. When sketching out possible character arcs, using core-value progressions, they're a helpful way to order complexity. Let's build another now.

The logical order to begin a flow chart on the value of greed is with the most natural state: hunger. Of course, satiety is also 'natural' and desirable, but hunger comes before satiety in the normal course of events. So the first half of our flow chart looks like this:

HUNGER → SATIETY

Greed is what we call it when a person overrides their natural satiety thresholds, be they physical or moral. Training themselves to ignore food-satiety mechanisms makes a person overeat whether they want to or not. Overriding moral satiety mechanisms makes a greedy person over-accumulate, though we all know money can't buy happiness. Greed follows when satiety is overridden. The two are strongly bonded, so a three-part progression could look like this:

HUNGER → SATIETY → GREED

You'll notice a trajectory developing now. This is a downward-heading story. Someone who has become greedy is dangerously warping the path of their life, and probably doesn't even know it yet. Which is tough, because unchecked greed can only end one way:

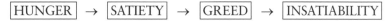

HUNGER → SATIETY → GREED → INSATIABILITY

The final position is where nothing works anymore. The natural mechanisms of satisfaction have been overridden to the point that they've broken entirely. Nothing can satisfy now, as the greedy enter a living torment.

This four-part progression is obviously powerful in narratives about people finding their feet in life, whether fictional or in life writing. A natural hunger for life and what it has to offer can become warped in the best of us, given economic pressures, often conflicting societal demands, and the baggage many carry from tough childhoods. It's a progression that can fuel a story of a basically good person's redemption, or a basically bad person's damnation.

But as we've already identified, with the poor little rich kid at the end of the last exercise, this progression can be played in different ways. Fruitful variations are possible, and can be suggested by jotting down a few more ideas on our flow chart.

The first step to exploring all our options with this flow-charted arc is to assign a 'charge', either positive or negative, to each of the arc's four positions. Hunger is a natural drive, a positive thing, so no problems there. Satiety is even better, as most of us would agree after a good meal. Only when natural satiety thresholds are overridden does a person enter negative territory. The final position is a living hell. So our flow chart now looks like this:

HUNGER (+) → SATIETY (++) → GREED (–) → INSATIABILITY (––)

Hunger is a natural good thing; satiety even better. Greed is a negative place to be in life; insatiability doubly so. So: positive, double-positive, negative, and double-negative. But human experience is so broad, and the human condition so infinitely fascinating in its processes, that most straightforward progressions of values, from positive to doubly negative, can be worked other ways, too, for narratives that grip readers. Let's look at how.

→ Designing original character arcs

Thinking of possible 'charges' on values, positive or negative, means we can start to work creatively with these values, and find other satisfying progressions to follow.

Hunger, with the means to satisfy it, is plainly positive, a healthy part of life. But many people aren't in a healthy place. As a supermarket trip in a peak period will show anyone, some people don't seem to know what satiety is. Their weekly shop is piled with desserts, sugared drinks, snack foods rich in fats and sugars, and they waddle as they trawl the aisles for more.

So what happened with these people? What's in their past that has them like this? What would you like to see happen in their future? Start the arc at greed, and a profound and positive story can fall into place:

| GREED | → | INSATIABILITY | → | HUNGER | → | SATIETY |

A person can become addicted to food for good reasons. People use food to self-medicate for all kinds of difficult mental conditions, many of which stem from childhood abuse. They may become obese or unproductive in life as a result; but overeating is a less immediately dangerous way for them to cope with unbearable feelings than other forms of self-harm.

Abused children grown into overeating adults have found a way to cope, then, rather than giving up the struggle. They may be using food to anaesthetize painful feelings, but it helps them cope with a life none would envy. When they're ready to face up to the abuse and get help for it, from outside or within, they may find better ways to soothe pain and exercise self-care. A positive arc can often derive from a negative opening position.

Starting the arc at greed for this character permits a story that opens with an actively deteriorating situation before intervention, midway through the progression, permits a positive and upward-trajectory ending. An abused child grown into an adult food addict could learn to identify their real 'hunger', by understanding what the abuse stole from them: a sense of safety, of security, of self, not to mention the chance to be a kid. When hunger for these is located, and satisfied in appropriate ways, this survivor can experience their rightful position in life for the first time:

| GREED (−) | → | INSATIABILITY (−−) | → | HUNGER (+) | → | SATIETY (++) |

→ Character arcs and core values: Locking the story together

Thinking laterally with standard character arcs can open up original and powerful stories. Another opening position on a greed progression would be to have someone who's been born into a greedy life, who has know nothing else.

A poor little rich-kid story could generate intrigue and vigour from a four-part progression that begins with greed. Perhaps the drinking this scion uses to cope with their strange position in life becomes an insatiability. It's easy for an alcoholic to end up on the street, but very tough for them to bootstrap themselves back to a fulfilling life.

GREED

for luxury, for more than their fellow humans have

↓

INSATIABILITY

for alcohol, to soothe the unnatural frustration of life in a privileged bubble

↓

HUNGER

for real life, when seen for the first-time from rock bottom

↓

SATIETY

as this character experiences the satisfaction of contributing to society for the first time

Moving from insatiability to hunger, and working again toward satiety experienced for the first time in life, permits a vigorous story of meaningful human change – one that can teeter at the 'top' of society, plunge to rock bottom, yet finish in the truly wealthy sector of humanity for the first time.

Developing core-value progressions in lockstep with character arcs generates both robustly classic stories and innovatively satisfying ones.

Exercise 29

CLASSIC ARC PROGRESSIONS

Can you think of a celebrity or athlete, or another big achiever you admire, whose life story follows this classic hunger progression? List a few of the other progressions we've worked with already (extra points if you don't have to turn back the pages to do this) and see if you can think of celebrities or other public-eye figures whose life trajectories show similar arcs.

_____

_____

_____

_____

_____

_____

_____

_____

_____

_____

_____

_____

_____

→ Character and backstory

Remember our skydiving chef from the start of this chapter? The gourmet who plays Dixieland saxophone when he isn't solving murders?

We're returning to him only now – to what a character needs to look like at the start of a piece, to get a reader's attention and hold it – because the bulk of this chapter's ideas need to inform your thinking before you start to sketch a single hair on your protagonist's head.

The key question an author must ask before creating character is not what kind of person do people want to read about but what kind of person can carry my four-part progression?

It's the qualities that can facilitate the four-part progression you've chosen that should be built into the backstory – all else is window-dressing, and should be cut. 'Backstory' as a term has entered the popular idiom, where it means 'anything that happened in the past'. But, for writers, it still means the events that equip – or cripple – a character for a particular story, helping them respond credibly and meaningfully to the slings and arrows of a four-part progression.

Exercise 30

BUILDING BACKSTORY

We've explored the tightly constructed yet complex character of James Bond already. His backstory featured in a couple of early Bond novels, but most people don't know it. Build a backstory for Bond that equips him with the qualities we've identified as key to the success of his character. The Sean Connery incarnation may be the most fruitful – find a way from a tough-knock life in the Glasgow tenements to life as an elite playboy assassin. Remember, we're not building a CV here or a Facebook timeline, but a backstory.

_____

_____

_____

_____

_____

_____

_____

Where to next?

We've seen how narrative is designed and constructed using basic building blocks. Now we'll move on to look at how the specifics of different kinds of narratives are delivered on the page. In the next chapter we'll cover fiction, but even if you're a memoirist or poet or dramatist, there'll be plenty of helpful ideas to develop your skill set and perspective.

Mastering dramatic structure is a key development for all writers, from feature journalists to free-verse poets (in Chapter 8 we'll look in detail at how poets use tight dramatic structures to fuel the extraordinary power in their work). In the next chapter, focusing on fiction, we'll explore the dramatic skills and techniques invaluable to all creative writers seeking to engage their readers.

Ideas and inspirations

▶ The key to making characters come alive on the page is to build contrast between initial characterization and developing deep character.

▶ Using the principle of Show Don't Tell in characterization and development engages readers in interpreting what they see on the page.

▶ Characters develop in meaningful ways, by design.

▶ Character arcs and core-value progressions can be combined by creative authors to build meaning, coherence and resonance in their work.

6

Fiction and drama

. . . .

In this chapter you will learn:

▶ Why dramatic structure and technique are central to writing both fiction and plays for stage, radio and screen.

▶ How the skills of the dramatist make even short stories and vignettes into powerful, fully developed creative pieces.

▶ How using dramatic 'acts' gives structure and pace to authors seeking to capitalize on their material's strengths.

▶ About using four-part character arcs and plot progressions within those three dramatic acts.

. . . .

→ Beginnings, middles and endings

Even the briefest of vignettes can be packed with developing power. Try this shortest of short stories, attributed by some to Ernest Hemingway:

> *For Sale: baby shoes, never worn.*

The set-up, achieved in the first two words, orients the reader to the world of the piece: this is a newspaper small ad. The middle of the piece – its third and fourth words – answers the question posed by the set-up. Its fifth and sixth words deliver the devastating climax.

Set-up, development, pay-off. As I hope you'll have noticed, that's a total of *three* movements, when our study of core-value progressions focused on *four* movements.

That's because three dramatic acts deliver three big progressions on an opening position – four positions in all. This is what people mean when they talk about the big twist at the end of Act 2 in a favourite TV episode or movie – they're talking about a big development on a story's value progression, delivered two-thirds of the way through the substance of the story.

Three acts is the standard structure for the telling of a tale, even in non-fiction such as memoir or travel writing. Blood-and-guts thrillers use three acts: so do nuanced literary novels. Accounts of human endeavour whether first-hand or in biography use a three-act structure, as do sensitive coming-of-age novels and hard-bitten detective stories. Radio plays use three acts, as do great works of drama and musicals alike.

Three acts is the basic template: set-up, development, resolution. Stories that need a lot of big cliff-hangers and twists sometimes use five acts – the romcom *Four Weddings and a Funeral*, for example, which takes its title from its five-act structure, or Shakespeare's plays.

But whether three-act or five-act in structure, the four-part value progression, underwriting what happens in core terms, drives the power and impact throughout.

Let's look at how a simple yet powerful short story works these on the page.

→ Case study: Dramatic structure in fiction

Our case study is 'The End of FIRPO in the World', the briefest story in short-fiction virtuoso Saunders's second published collection.

ACT 1: SET-UP

The story hits the ground running, literally:

The boy on the bike flew by the chink's house, and the squatty-body's house, and the house where the dead guy had rotted for five days...

Offensive language is up in our faces immediately. It hits us square – the slap is almost palpable – but immediately it's tempered as we realize this is a kid speaking. 'Squatty-body' sounds like one of those private phrases that little kids make up, and the fascination with a house where a death occurred locates this firmly as the first-person of a young child. Consequently, we're forced to recast the automatic recoil produced by the first words.

The author has engaged us powerfully already. We know that kids don't learn racism, even casual racism, from nowhere. Already, we're into the world of the story, and thinking. The offensive language that this kid uses sounds like part of the vocabulary he's been taught; we realize at once that this child does not have a happy home life.

In this context, his interest in the five-day corpse suddenly seems healthy – we're glad this kid is still able to take an interest in normal kid-things. The first verb of the sentence is recast, too; we hope this kid can indeed fly from whoever is teaching him racist vocabulary.

Our sympathies, powerfully evoked, are deepened by the second half of this first sentence:

> *… remembering that the chink had once called him nasty, the squatty-body had once called the cops when he'd hit her cat with a lug nut on a string, the chick in the dead guy's house had once asked if he, Cody, ever brushed his teeth.*

It's plain now that this is a hurt child. A healthy kid would brush off aspersions cast by strangers, but a wounded kid – striving to preserve themselves in trying circumstances – would mind very much if someone called them 'nasty'. Children from chaotic homes are deeply shamed by others highlighting their impoverished appearance or hygiene. And hurt children are known to act out by hurting animals. The horrible detail of the lug nut is both disturbing and pitiful – it's a meagre toy for a kid to cobble together, a scrapyard conker.

We realize, by the end of the first sentence, that this is a tough, gritty story about a kid from the kind of home where racist and demeaning language is standard vocabulary. Sympathy for Cody is evoked in a surprising way, with shocking information about his traumatized acting-out. The first half of the opening sentence is a visceral set-up; its second half a visceral pay-off. Saunders's fidelity to realism – to what an abused child actually looks like playing on the street – has drawn us into the world of his story and powerfully engaged us.

The paragraphs that follow develop our identification with Cody. Despite what's waiting for him at home, he's out on his bike, living in the moment, enjoying himself. A few brief lines, as Cody careers around the neighbourhood – a sequence that makes us feel both deeply nostalgic and keen to get on a bicycle right now – set the foundation of this story, and secure our engagement, in just a few hundred words. The set-up phase of the three-act structure is complete already.

ACT 1 – OPENING POSITIONS, ARC AND PLOT

As we've seen, storytellers work with four core-value positions, but usually just three dramatic acts. In the next three exercises we'll analyse how three acts are used, in this short story, to deliver four core-value positions that develop and resolve Cody's character arc.

So to begin: Which value does this story begin by examining? Where is Cody on its four-part progression through the opening sequence of this story?

_____

_____

I think Saunders is using a particular but important kind of loyalty as his core value. Cody is a child in difficult circumstances trying to retain his sense of being a kid. Though we're confronted straight away with evidence of a disadvantaged and possibly dangerous home life, Cody is out on his bike riding like the wind – significantly, the very first verb the author uses to introduce Cody is 'to fly'. We want this kid to have wings, to stay loyal to himself and the kind of carefree kid he wants to be, despite what happens at home.

But we can see that, for all his efforts, Cody is caught in split allegiance here. He wants to be a good kid, but the world is not letting him. Instead, he's wrenched by dilemma, in this opening sequence, torn between what his abusive home life requires him to be – a robot who needs no care – and the child he can't help being.

→ Act 2: Development

The middle act comes next. This is where what's established in the set-up is developed, deepening our engagement with the story.

For Cody, this development consists of riding past the home of prosperous schoolmates, the Dalmeyer brothers. Powerful shame is evoked, as Cody remembers a play visit there, and being humiliated for not knowing which brands of their sports equipment were meant for rough play in the street, and which expensive brands were reserved for when the Dalmeyers hosted play dates with their affluent friends.

It's a horribly insightful glimpse – a reminder, no doubt, for many – of the world of childhood hierarchies. Cody has gamely learned the sports that the privileged kids enjoy, but is shamed for not being able to differentiate standard brands of equipment from expensive. We realize that all brands seem expensive to this kid, as the author takes us deep into Cody's world by showing us a nuanced, authentic expression of disadvantage in early life. The sequence concludes with Cody fantasizing an elaborate revenge on the Dalmeyers for their snobbery; the ingenuity of his plans – to back up their drains and flood their perfect home with sewage – evokes our admiration, and deepens our engagement with this child protagonist.

Mid-act, the perspective shifts suddenly and dramatically. It's time for the author to show us the kind of home Cody is heading back to, so the narrator pulls back suddenly to a bird's-eye view, before zooming sharply back in to Cody's consciousness, redoubling and intensifying the focus as we learn of the troubles in this little boy's life.

His own small house predates the modern dwellings Cody has just passed: it smells 'like cat pee and hamburger blood'. Waiting there are his mother and her boyfriend: 'Daryl, that dick'. Immediately, we learn the reason for Cody's disparaging assessment, and the meaning of the mystifying word in the story's title. FIRPO, we're told, is 'the word Daryl used to describe anything he, Cody, did that was bad or dorky'.

Both adults use this silly word as a term of abuse for the child, we learn. Sometimes they tousle his hair as they say it; sometimes they physically abuse him. Far from comforting her child, Cody's mother follows this treatment by mocking him, about both his weight and his tearfulness.

Cody is not even permitted the concept of crying: he uses his abusive parents' phrase, 'making the nosehole sound', to refer to his own weeping. It's a horrible development, as we realize how far this poor child has been forced to become estranged from his own emotions. Again, Saunders's fidelity to realism, to how parental abuse plays out in practice – not just ill-treating children, but mocking them for their wounds – is augmented by his meticulously structured storytelling.

 *Exercise 32*

ACT 2 – DEVELOPMENT

What is the progression in Act 2 of this story? What do we learn about this kid's life and what's happening in it? Which one-word phrase represents the next development on the core value, the next progression in Cody's arc?

In Act 2 of this story, we learn how Cody is traduced by betrayal. We learn how both of the adults in his life hurt and mock him, piling mockery upon insult upon abuse. Cody is not just a child who isn't having his needs met; he's being actively hurt.

Our worst fears are swiftly confirmed by the author; and, again, to force deeper engagement, he involves us anew with his story. When he introduces the term 'the nosehole sound', we're tempted to think it's a kid's nonsense language; with its second and third repetitions, however, we're left in no doubt – this is the phrase his abusive parents use to shame Cody for weeping.

We realize that physical and emotional abuse have so damaged this child that he has been forced to see his own natural responses to ill-treatment as gross and shameful – 'making the nosehole sound' is how he describes his own misery now. The story progresses from split allegiance to betrayal, as we realize Cody's lot in life: this child has been horribly betrayed.

➜ Act 3: Resolution

The cut to Act 3 comes as Cody finishes his lap of the block and passes the Dalmeyer house a second time. His revenge fantasy kicks in again, and he doesn't notice a car. Suddenly, he's flying across the street – we're reminded of the very first verb of the story – while his bike is slammed so hard against a tree that its frame bends around the trunk. We realize, in the space of half a sentence, that Cody has suddenly moved from being a child who is coping with a tough life to a child with mere seconds to live.

The narrator is already inside Cody's consciousness, so we hear his last thoughts as he dies. First, he panics about the blood on his shoes, anticipating how Daryl will punish and shame him. Welling shame triggers him to relive another shameful moment when he slipped and fell during a school play and when, afterward, even his teacher was as mean as his mother. This is a child who's been cruelly betrayed in life at every turn, we realize, and now he's dying.

An old man runs out of a house to cradle the little boy as the life leaves his body. The only words Cody can find for such an act of basic humanity are, again, those of his abusive parents: his dying mind mocks the old man's physical appearance. The old man's attempts to reassure the child that he needn't be scared of death elicit only more of the abusive parents' mean-minded language. Cody has been the target of it for so long that it's the only language he knows now. So even as the old man tries to gently talk the dying child out of the world, Cody has only the language and perspectives of his abusers with which to respond:

> *What a Holy Roller. What a FIRPO. A Holy Roller FIRPO stickman with hairy nips and plus his breath smelled like coffee.*

We realize that this child has been so ill-treated that his ability to receive comfort, even when dying, has been broken beyond repair. The pathos of Saunders's deeply affecting story is almost unbearable through its final lines, as Cody dies, fantasizing about his mother graciously accepting his apology 'for having been such a FIRPO son'. The narrator steps back from Cody's consciousness only when it's extinguished. The line that follows, the final line of the story, runs:

You are beautiful, beautiful, the stickman kept saying, long after the boy had stopped thrashing, God loves you, you are beautiful in His sight.

A story that began with the ugliest of language ends in poetry.

ACT 3 – STORY CLIMAX

 If betrayal follows split allegiance, what's next for Cody? What happens in the story to conclude it? How does this follow the progression so far?

SPLIT ALLEGIANCE → BETRAYAL → ?

_____

_____

_____

_____

_____

_____

_____

_____

_____

_____

_____

_____

The third act of stories must achieve the final position on both the character arc and the core progression. Act 3 is the end of the line, quite literally in this story.

As Cody dies, he is caught in self-betrayal. He has been hurt so badly in his short life that he can't even accept human comfort as he leaves it. The little boy dies alone, despite the old man trying to comfort him.

His mother and stepfather have damaged Cody so deeply that, even as he bleeds out on to the road, he must scorn the human comfort offered. Instead, he disappears inside himself, fantasizing about finally finding a way to make his abusive mother accept him.

The kid who was trying to be a kid at the start of the story has not had a chance; Saunders's deeply moving story is a tale of everyday common-or-garden child abuse, powered with three dramatic acts to deliver a devastating four-part progression.

→ Drama: Distilling reality

To tell Cody's story, and to tell it as powerfully as possible, Saunders didn't show us Cody suffering at home. He showed us Cody out on his bike, trying to fly, trying to transcend his life.

The author distilled all of Cody's world, in this short story, into the last couple of minutes of a kid's short life. The reality of an abused child's existence, and of great weight borne on young shoulders, is condensed into the simple action of riding a bike once around a neighbourhood block. Escalating dramatic structure and progressive escalation of a core progression freight that simple bike ride with devastating power and meaning.

Creative writing is not about simply taking a chunk of reality and putting it on the page. Very little happens in reality for long periods; this is a state most of us desire, 'a quiet life'. But effective writing can't just be about the times when life is, by contrast, unquiet – the crises big and small all of us must face from time to time. Authors use core-value progressions, driving character arcs, to describe the meaningful changes that these crises provoke, whether they're sudden and sharp crises or festering for years. To create such meaning in our work, creative writers focus on a distilled reality.

Exercise 34

DISTILLING REALITY

Consider the entire lifespan of each of the following:

1. A successful entrepreneur who, speeding between meetings, kills a child

2. A tree that destroys a house when it falls in a hurricane

3. An eighteenth-century watermill in a coastal valley

Now make three big events in each lifespan. The watermill could be built to settle a feud, or escalate one; in its golden years it could generate enough income for a poor family to educate their child, and see them make a great contribution to society; a century later its ruins could be used by smugglers, or runaways, or deserters.

The entrepreneur could be bringing water to Third World communities or selling landmines to local warlords. The tree must have been around a long time, and seen plenty of people around it, to cause that kind of damage when it falls. Remember to build in ways to show rather than tell.

1. **A successful entrepreneur who, speeding between meetings, kills a child**

_____

_____

_____

_____

_____

_____

_____

_____

_____

_____

_____

_____

_____

_____

_____

_____

_____

2. A tree that destroys a house when it falls in a hurricane

_____

_____

_____

_____

_____

_____

3. An eighteenth-century watermill in a coastal valley

_____

_____

_____

_____

_____

_____

_____

_____

_____

_____

_____

_____

_____

So what kind of stories are you telling? What are the core values highlighted by your successive choices in each of the three stories?

1. _____

_____

_____

_____

_____

_____

_____

2. _____

_____

_____

_____

_____

_____

_____

3. _____

_____

_____

_____

_____

_____

_____

Finally, can you trace progressions in that core value in the kinds of stories that your choices suggest? Try to trace arrows on to your answers above.

→ Fiction: The novel

That was another tough exercise, but we're gearing up now to explore what many see as the ultimate creative expression: the novel.

There are few other disciplines that require so many years of preparation – in order to form an authorial worldview and skill set – and so many hundreds if not thousands of hours of work to produce a single artefact. Novelists are rightly respected, both among the general populace and among creative writers. They put the hours in.

Yet they're working, at heart, with the same simple numbers we've discussed so far – three dramatic acts; four-part value progressions. Let's look at how it plays out in practice in a classic novel.

→ Case study: Progressions, arcs and acts in the novel

George Orwell's *Nineteen Eighty-Four* is a novel whose prescience and power continue to resonate with readers the world over.

Written as a heartfelt warning, at the start of the 'cold war' between the US and Soviet superpowers, Orwell's novel envisions a high-tech world that enslaves its citizens: a dystopia. In this future world, a political revolution that began in fellow feeling has ended, as in Soviet Russia, with brutal repression. An interactive screen is installed in every dwelling, both to feed constant lies to members of the public and individually to scrutinize and harangue them. It's become a crime, punishable by torture and brainwashing, to question anything at all in life.

The novel's hero is Winston Smith, a man whose job is to erase the past. Working at a government ministry, Winston spends all day rewriting old news reports: ones that contradict the 'truth' as peddled currently. Winston's job is both high-risk and soul-destroying: if an assassinated politician needs to be airbrushed from an old photo of big cheeses, and the caption rewritten, Winston does it. If production forecasts published a year ago have fallen far short, Winston must amend the forecast to make the shortfall look like a bounty. The hero's work is powerfully at odds with his inner nature.

He's a man who longs to be free. He wants to live and love and experience. He wants to be true to himself as a man, even as he's forced to erase truth for a living. As with James Bond, strongly-bonded surface and depth are established in the characterization as Orwell's novel opens.

ACT 1

Orwell is working with the same core value for his hero as Saunders used with Cody: loyalty. Winston opens at the same position on the value as Cody does: split allegiance. Winston Smith is caught between his own humanity and a state that seeks brutally to suppress it.

But this is distilled reality. We don't see Winston's years of grey grind playing out before us; they're shown by implication. Instead, the action begins with Winston doing the unthinkable: writing, secretly.

On the black market he has purchased, at great personal risk, a journal and a pen, and hidden them away. In the novel's first scene he allows himself the unimaginable transgression of putting his thoughts on to paper.

As we've explored, the most straightforward progression on the value of loyalty looks like this:

Like George Saunders in the story analysed above, Orwell begins the progression for his protagonist at split allegiance. But Winston is trying hard to find a way to be loyal to his own sense of self, and there's a positive progression to come.

He's been spurred into writing – a capital crime in this dystopia – by a fleeting moment of human contact, the first Winston has experienced in decades. At a public event, in the midst of a seething crowd, a senior official made eye-contact with him, and for a second Winston felt a kindred spirit. Neither man could acknowledge the other further at the time, but the incident was Winston's first glimmer of hope in a life largely devoid of it.

The official's name is O'Brien, and he's so high in the pecking-order that no one knows what his job is – yet this man has shared a few seconds of seditious eye-contact with Winston. As the novel opens, he is feeling for the first time that he may not be alone in life.

The first act develops this feeling, ultimately to reinforce it. Winston meets a similarly seditious young woman, Julia, and begins a passionate clandestine affair. For the first time in his life he feels like a man. Though everything he does – meeting Julia, making love, sharing pillow-talk full of deeply human longing – is punishable by certain death for both Winston and his lover, the protagonist begins to feel like the kind of man his soul demands to be. Winston moves in Act 1 of this novel from a stasis of split allegiance to loyalty to self in thought, deed and human longing for life:

$$\boxed{\text{SPLIT ALLEGIANCE}} \rightarrow \boxed{\text{LOYALTY}}$$

ACT 2

Winston's character arc has made an enormous progression. From feeling traduced in everything he does, he's found a way to be himself. Split allegiance, with its push–pull stasis, has been overcome as Winston finds loyalty to himself in his actions, and the human emotions they evoke. Secretly, he rents a hidden love-nest, and in stolen hours he and Julia share a fantasy domesticity as the lovers and partners they can never be in the real world.

Naturally their pillow-talk turns to other fantasies: overthrow of this brutal system, and the possibility that there might be others like them. Officially, there is indeed an underground rebellion, led by a hate-figure called Emmanuel Goldstein. But both lovers have to conclude that Goldstein is a fabrication, a cartoon drawn by the State to justify its repression and refract its subjects' natural dissatisfaction. When food is scarce, Goldstein's rebels are to blame. When shoddily-made shoes let in rain, that's down to Goldstein too. Surely, any thought of an organized resistance to this tyranny is fantasy?

The mid-act climax powers the progression forward. O'Brien, the government bigwig who shared a silent moment with Winston early in Act 1, re-enters the frame. Out of the blue, he stops Winston in the office canteen, compliments him on his work, offers to lend him a helpful book if Winston will drop by his quarters that evening. There, at O'Brien's luxury apartment, the first building Winston has seen without room-by-room surveillance, the powerful man tells Winston something astounding.

Goldstein exists. So does his resistance movement. The book O'Brien lends Winston is actually Goldstein's manifesto, a secretly circulated analysis of how power is enforced and why. Winston's progression to a position of loyalty is reinforced – now he has a partner, a cause and a movement of men to be loyal to.

But at the Act 2 climax, the next logical progression kicks into step. Julia and Winston read Goldstein's book to each other, and discuss it passionately, fantasizing about what an overthrown state could mean for humanity. It feels like they're living in a new kind of reality, blissful and hopeful while it can last.

Then the old reality reasserts itself. As Winston and Julia share an intimate moment in their secret love-nest, a voice barks suddenly from a hidden microphone. Storm troopers kick in the window and door, and flood the tiny attic room.

ACT 3

From a position of reinforced loyalty, this sudden action sends the value progression into a sickening lurch:

SPLIT ALLEGIANCE → LOYALTY → BETRAYAL

O'Brien is the betrayer. It turns out there's a reason no one knows his actual job title: he's chief torturer for this brutally repressive state.

In this novel's final act, he physically tortures and emotionally manipulates Winston in ways that, after Abu Ghraib and Guantanamo, seem horribly prescient. By the end of the novel, Winston is broken and brainwashed. He's a man who accepts the State's lies without question. Julia endures a similar fate and, when at the end of the novel they meet again, they have nothing to say to each other – except to agree that when you've been made to betray someone else under torture, you feel numb toward them afterward.

Winston began as a man determined to live life, not numb himself out to it in order to survive. Now, after torture and brainwashing, the only thing he's able to feel is love for his oppressors: the novel ends with him weeping with adoration at a propaganda broadcast. His dehumanization, by an inhuman state, moves him to the end of the line.

The final, crushing step on this powerful value progression, constructed to warn of the dangers of technology-drenched, dehumanized regimes, plays out in the only way it can now:

SPLIT ALLEGIANCE → LOYALTY → BETRAYAL → SELF-BETRAYAL

→ Mastering the novel

Novels are complex beasts whose authorship requires a wide variety of advanced writing skills and a lot of stamina. There's no easy route to writing one. But, at heart, all successful novels play out coherent core progressions. They're concerned with human values, and how these find expression; their value progressions echo those we experience – or fear or long for – in real life.

In *Nineteen Eighty-Four* the four possible positions on the value of loyalty drive a powerful character arc and a resounding, engaging story. The value progression directs the plot. From the stasis of split allegiance, caught between inner loyalty and outward conformity, Winston Smith finds loyalty to self, and to Julia. Together, they fantasize about a whole movement of people, just like them, hiding their sedition and working for a human future. Their inner loyalty to their inner selves is reinforced by outward expression – to each other, and with the promise of being to claim, and feel, loyalty to a whole secret resistance.

Then comes crushing betrayal, and its logical end point for Winston: the rock bottom of self-betrayal. In Orwell's cautionary tale, the forces of evil win.

Whatever the forces in your own novel, whether half-finished on your hard drive or still scribbled on notes in a drawer, revisiting your material now will pay a big dividend. Try this exercise to return to your novel with fresh eyes.

Exercise 35

DRAMA AND THE NOVEL

If you're not working on a novel of your own, use the following scenario for this exercise: a young person of your own gender moves from a small town to a big city and finds acceptance and a sense of identity, despite the usual vicissitudes of a twenty-something's professional and personal life.

 Use incidents from your own past to sketch this story out briefly, before you begin the exercise. Include enough incident to power an opening movement, a middle section, and a concluding movement to the story: you'll need set-up, development and resolution. If you're stuck, think of the set-up phase as the move to the city and what triggers it; the development phase as the joys of freedom versus the strains of trying to make a living in the rat-race city; and the resolution phase as what happens to make your protagonist either stay in the city or leave.

1. Where is your protagonist, whether single or 'multiple', at the start of the story? What value is your story exploring here?

_____

_____

_____

_____

_____

_____

_____

_____

_____

_____

2. What happens when this value is progressed? For example, after a big move to the city, the protagonist will probably experience both freedom (usually in their personal life) and restriction (usually financial in nature). This usually progresses the core value in this kind of *Bildungsroman*, or 'coming-of-age' novel, from a relatively simple opening position to a more complex, 'middle-ground' position. For example, a small-town kid who thinks the big city will be nothing but the chance to build a career, and meet a mate to build a life in tandem, could find themselves in a world of casual hook-ups and terminal career uncertainty.

_____

_____

_____

_____

_____

_____

_____

_____

_____

_____

_____

_____

_____

_____

3. Now comes something to break the stasis. In our move-to-the-city story, someone whom the protagonist thought was a casual hook-up becomes, in Act 2, the person they want to spend their life with. But at the Act 2 climax, through no real fault of their own, suddenly our protagonist is unemployed, their dreams in tatters. Now the only prudent option is to return to the small town, left behind with such high hopes. How does this value progression break down now?

_____

_____

_____

_____

_____

_____

_____

_____

_____

_____

_____

_____

4. In Act 3 of an up-ending story the protagonist finds new resources of courage and character and defeats the forces of antagonism. In a down-ending story, like Orwell's discussed above, the protagonist's sense of self is broken by the antagonist.

→ For an up ending to our move-to-the-city story, the protagonist could compromise on what they realize they truly need in life: their soulmate, not big-city money or a fast-paced lifestyle. Thus, they find a way to take their city experiences to somewhere life is more affordable.

For a down ending, it doesn't work out for these two. The forces that made them meet as casual hook-ups send them back into that city world. The demands of the rat race dictate their behaviour.

So what's your chosen resolution? What does the whole of the value progression you've worked with here look like? Draw it out with arrows.

_____

_____

_____

_____

_____

_____

_____

_____

_____

_____

Where to next?

We've explored how fiction uses core-value progressions, delivered with dramatic acts, to structure and fuel its power. We've analysed how the basic pattern of set-up, development and resolution of both a plot and its primary character arc is driven by the four-part progression technique that writers use to map human change on to plots that can engage and satisfy.

Now we'll look at how the same techniques and perspectives are applied in life writing to secure and sustain a reader's interest. From blogging, to writing a memoir or biography, to keeping a journal, we'll use our understanding of drama in narrative to explore how life writers of every kind inject intrigue and power into their work.

First, let's summarize what we've learned in this chapter:

▶ Even the shortest of short fiction can exploit the three-part dramatic progression of set-up, development and pay-off/resolution.

▶ The first dramatic act of novel or short story establishes the opening positions of both the central character arc and the central plot progression.

▶ The second dramatic act of a fictional piece develops both character arc and plot, typically to an 'all is lost' moment at the act climax that slingshots the action into its final movement.

▶ The concluding dramatic act gives fiction authors opportunities to generate satisfaction with surprise – making a typically negative value into a positive, for example – to build powerfully affecting resolutions, for good or ill.

7

Life writing

In this chapter you will learn:

▶ How to 'work with what you know', using your own experiences to create satisfying dramatic progressions in a narrative.

▶ Why the life-writing sector is a vibrant place to work, for people from all walks of life.

▶ How to build power and page-turning readability into life-writing narratives.

▶ How to structure and pace life stories.

→ Writing life

Life writing spurs creativity for many people from all walks of life. From journal writing to blogging, to making sense of one's own experiences by writing about them, to recording the memories of elderly loved-ones, life writing gives authors the chance to explore their creativity using material that has direct emotional resonance for them.

In doing so, they develop the skill to which all creative arts aspire: turning an author's complex perspectives into an experience that can be shared. By working with material that comes freighted with resonance – the fabric of their own lives, those of loved-ones or ancestors, or of historical figures that fascinate them – life writers from bloggers to literary biographers practise their art in the glowing heart of creativity's forge.

Life writing for many begins with studying their own lives, or those around them, and developing their observations and thoughts in writing – whether in a journal, a blog or in a creative piece 'drawn from life'. Let's try an exercise that works with material you know better than anyone.

Exercise 36

'WORKING WITH WHAT YOU KNOW'

Choose an incident from your life where you stood your ground and took the consequences, for better or worse. It could be a work dispute; it could be a family disagreement; it could be an everyday incident that took place as you were growing up or in your personal life. The force against which you stood your ground could even be yourself, in overcoming the legacy of a difficult past for example, or a regrettable relationship choice.

If you're stuck, pick a 'stand-your-ground' moment from a movie or TV drama; a couple that spring to my mind are *Ferris Bueller's Day Off*, where a neglected kid hoofs in the headlamps of his father's Ferrari, or *The Sopranos*, where a mobster's daughter evolves a compromise between her sense of self and her family's criminality. Unless you remember your key scene or scenes well, revisit your chosen material – YouTube probably has it – before you try this exercise.

As you can see from the screen examples given, in this exercise you can work with a single resonant event or a process. Either way, try to boil down the basics of what happens into a sequential list of bullet points – but remember, sequential doesn't necessarily mean chronological. Order events in the way that carries most meaning for you.

_____

_____

_____

Next, use the space below to map emotions on to those bullet-pointed events. Try to stick to single words or short phrases, but record the essence of your feelings at each point in your bulleted progression. Don't think about what you'd expect a character in a book to feel about each event, concentrate on what *you* felt – or feel now as you recall what happened.

_____

_____

_____

_____

_____

_____

_____

_____

_____

_____

_____

_____

_____

_____

_____

_____

_____

_____

_____

Now identify the highs and lows across your sequence of emotional bullet points above, and mark them in – use a plus sign for high points in the process, a minus for the more difficult parts. If you can, try to reflect escalations by using multiple plus or minus signs, as your chosen situation escalated to resolution.

For example, if I was working with the example of Ferris Bueller's buddy kicking the car, my answer above might look something like this:

▶ The kid voices his frustration at being neglected (+)

▶ The kid talks insightfully about how this neglect affects him (++)

▶ The kid vents anger at this treatment by kicking his father's prized possession (+++)

▶ The Ferrari rolls off its stand and through the wall, smashing into a gully (––––)

▶ The kid resolves to explain why he kicked the car rather than simply take the consequences (++++)

Another example – a work situation most of us have experienced:

▶ I noticed something at my job which shouldn't have been happening

▶ I put up with its effects on me for a while

▶ I decided enough was enough and spoke up

▶ Things seemed to improve and I felt I'd done my job

▶ I got stabbed in the back

I'm sure you can fill in the progression of plus and minus signs yourself in this example; now try it on your own progression above.

So, were you able to define and grade the emotions in this exercise, as well as locate them? If you were able to get back into the memory of standing your ground, or become immersed in your screen-drama scenario again, then you may well have been able to locate the emotional processes you went through when these things were experienced and reflected upon for the first time. It's this emotional process that will engage a reader with 'the heart of your story' when you use the tools and perspectives of creative writing to transform emotional experience into narrative.

But it may be that your chosen example above was so fraught with complicating factors that you couldn't see a coherent pattern develop. If that was the case, try this exercise again with a simple example from a favourite movie or TV show – something simple and powerful like the Ferris Bueller scene. This exercise practises the discipline that life writers excel in – mapping the detail and depth of life as it's lived into a narrative that a reader can share. Getting to the emotional heart of material is a core skill, and it's one we'll explore and practise through this chapter.

→ Life writing in the market

Ours is the age of self-definition through wordsmith creativity. From texting to tweeting to updating Facebook statuses on the move, technology has turned writing about the self into a rewarding part of many people's everyday social and family lives.

At the other end of the life-writing scale, big literary biographies and memoirs have won massive readerships by experimenting with the genre, from David Niven's *The Moon's a Balloon* and more recent Hollywood memoirs, to inventive biographies of Dickens and Eliot by present-day literary heavyweights.

Yet despite this discipline's soaring popularity – most creative-writing faculties run life writing courses today, while life writers bring their enthusiasm to many local writers' groups – it's traditionally got a bad press. Germaine Greer once called biography 'pre-digested carrion'. George Eliot considered it 'a disease of English literature'. Oscar Wilde remarked that 'every great man has his disciples, but it is usually Judas who writes the biography' – this last quote was revived in literary circles not long ago by a portrait of the great novelist Iris Murdoch as she suffered from Alzheimer's in her last years. Her husband wrote it, as an unflinching study of a terrible disease, but some didn't want to remember a great artist in that way.

Memoirs often fare no better. Consider the snobbishness toward 'misery lit', memoirs of abuse and suffering that plainly resonate with millions of readers, who are perhaps seeking to understand their own difficult pasts. But, recently, the popularity of life writing among local groups and university students has begun to be reflected in the bestseller market. Big literary biographies will always make headlines, but books like Kate Summerscale's *The Suspicions of Mr Whicher* – a biography focusing not on a whole life, but a single back-country police investigation – score surprise smash hits with readers responding to new approaches in a fluid and innovative genre.

So who reads life writing, and what are they reading for?

→ Raising the roof

The word 'detective' comes from the Latin for 'to unroof' – to lift the slates and shingles and peer at the humanity within. Even when writing about themselves, this is what the life writer must do – lift the roof and peer, just like a hard-bitten detective.

But first we must know what we're looking at. Most of us could produce a reasonably adequate summation of major events in our lives, given time and a few sheets of paper – things that happened which made us how we are today.

These are the official landmarks in our personal journeys, but we know that such lists of achievements, joys and perhaps heartaches are just the skeleton of the whole story. To put flesh on to these bare bones, we must move into the realm of the less documented: the struggles behind the achievements, the long-built emotional foundations that underpin – or undermine – the potential for joy, or for recovery from heartbreak.

Exercise 37

DISTILLING THE ESSENCE OF A LIFE STORY

Write your life as a country and western song. If you can't bear country, substitute the old-school blues here. The format is:

→ I was born and raised in [X]

→ Where life was sweet/harsh because of [Y]

→ I had [Z] and maybe [*], too

→ But then [A] happened

→ And [B] came along

→ Now I've got [C] and [D]

→ But I still miss that [Y], [Z] and [!]

Fill in the blanks for your life story in song:

→ X:_____

→ Y: _____

→ Z:_____

→ *: _____

→ A:_____

→ B:_____

→ C:_____

→ D:_____

Now you've sorted out the verse, what's the chorus? What's the message of this song? Which core value does this narrative ditty examine? Jot some thoughts down here:

_____

_____

_____

_____

_____

_____

_____

_____

_____

_____

_____

_____

→ Looking within: Character arcs and plot progressions

A great sea-change transformed the art of painting centuries ago, when artists began trying to capture the soul of a subject, not just the physical appearance. The life writer's job is to do just the same – to look beyond the 'outward face' shown to the world and see the real human processes at work.

So, having raised the roof on a life, the creative writer's job is to make sense of what's within. In earlier chapters on drama and fiction, we looked at the kind of core values, and value progressions, that drive narratives and give them coherence and power. They don't limit or pigeonhole the expression of experience, but help the resonance and meaning of life – of the jumble of striving and compromise we'd see, were we literally to lift joists and shingles and look within – to cohere and come alive on the page.

Writers do this because readers don't want jumble. In a story about a terrible personal betrayal, for example, they don't necessarily want a supplementary romance – or similar subplot narrative, restoring the protagonist's zest for life – to sweeten the pill. What they want, if they're prepared to read about betrayal, is a full narrative treatment of the issue. They want to see how a terrible personal betrayal actually plays out in life:

▶ **split allegiance**, as pressures build in the run-up to a betrayal – or divide loyalties in its aftermath

▶ **new loyalty**, perhaps – as with a concerned spouse who, after an eye-opening experience, decides to put self and security first

▶ yet **self-betrayal** might follow, if that spouse gives up on their resolve, and tries to follow the path of least resistance – loyalty despite negative experience – rather than being clear-eyed about where they stand.

Life writing examines themes in the same way that country or blues songs – and most popular music – have a 'message'. Analysing a song's 'message', or a movie's message or a novel's, is a way to think about core values. Thinking about narrative material in this way – whether life writing or any literary creativity – is how authors satisfy readers hungry for rewarding reading experiences.

Structuring material for greatest core-value coherence is how creative authors build page-turning readability into their work. Using core-value sequences as basic templates to progress a narrative – in life or travel writing, in fiction or drama, in poetry or a newspaper interview – is a writerly approach that seeks not to impose subheadings on life, but rather foreground the coherence and meaning beneath the surface complication.

⏱ Exercise 38

STRUCTURING LIFE

Imagine that you're reading about life writing because you're getting over a painful break-up, and you want to find closure by writing about it. Your backstory, whether you're newly single as a teenager or a grandparent, is a not unusual one:

→ You fell in love

→ Life got in the way

→ True colours started to come out

→ You tried to make it work, but you were the only one trying to change

→ You don't want to make the same mistakes again

Using the example of a betrayal progression that preceded this exercise, can you build a coherent arc by fleshing out this story? Here's an example of how stages one to five above might look, built as a value progression on the theme of loyalty and betrayal:

→ Loyalty to self, in fulfilling the need for a deep emotional relationship

→ Split allegiance, between partner and work and/or other pressures

→ Betrayal, when what you thought was for ever turned out not to be

→ Temporary self-betrayal perhaps, as you sacrifice your needs to try to save the relationship

→ New loyalty to self, older and wiser

 So let's try putting some flesh on the bones of this progression. If you've never got your heart broken, try the exercise for a teenager who thinks they have fallen in love, or a grandparent who knows they once did. Either way, try to flesh out each of these five stages with ideas for how to play these progressions on the page: start sketching, if you can, a few scenes or progressions of scenes, as the truth unfolds for the protagonist, with climaxes and maybe even a cliff-hanger or two if you're feeling fancy. Take some time for this exercise, and maybe revisit it a few times as ideas strike.

1. _____

_____

_____

_____

_____

_____

_____

_____

_____

_____

_____

_____

_____

_____

_____

_____

_____

_____

_____

_____

_____

_____

_____

_____

_____

_____

_____

2. _____

3. _____

_____

_____

_____

_____

_____

_____

_____

_____

_____

_____

_____

_____

_____

_____

_____

_____

_____

_____

_____

_____

4. _____

_____

_____

_____

_____

_____

_____

_____

_____

_____

_____

_____

_____

_____

_____

_____

_____

_____

_____

_____

_____

_____

_____

_____

_____

_____

_____

_____

5. _____

_____

_____

_____

_____

_____

_____

_____

_____

_____

_____

_____

_____

_____

_____

_____

_____

_____

_____

_____

_____

I hope that began to flow, once you got into it. Mapping value progressions out at the planning stage of writing helps authors create a solid dramatic structure for their material, naturally foregrounding ideas that will stand out on the page. Putting a typical human experience – such as attraction/coupling/growing apart/breaking up – into terms that writers can use, when we begin to sketch out narratives, helps us think objectively about human experience when we raise the roof on a life, be it our own or someone else's.

→ Distilling the essence of life

So what happens in creative life writing isn't about representing the *entirety* of the subject – imagine a poem about a tree that tells you everything there is to know about its species and lifespan, for example – but about making it meaningful by distilling its essence. Just as painters try to capture the souls of their subjects, distilling their essence into a *Mona Lisa* smile or a Francis Bacon howl, so creative writers try to capture the soul of life, the deep meaning behind its everyday jumble of conflicting demands and emotions.

Even journal writers and bloggers can benefit from thinking in terms of core values. The processes they represent are the fabric of life all around us, its escalations and surprises and reversals. Drawing meaning from the constant flow and eddy of life means using structured ways of thinking to build resonance for readers unconnected to that life.

Exercise 39

STRUCTURE AND PACE IN LIFE WRITING

In this exercise, we'll try working with different life stories as we build structure and inject pace into their telling. Consider the following three biographies:

1. An Afghanistan veteran adjusting to life after service

2. Amateur athlete wins Olympic gold

3. A big lottery winner ten years down the line

What is the first thing that strikes you as you ponder how these life stories could be written? Where is the pivotal point in each of these protagonist's personal timelines? If you're a poet, think in poetic terms; if you're a dramatist or fiction writer, in your own terms similarly.

1. _____

2. _____

3. _____

The life-changing event is the pivotal point of each story. The tour of duty in Afghanistan, the Olympic Games, and the big lottery draw.

Simple enough. Now, where in each scenario's timeline should this event be placed, in a piece of creative writing intended to engage a reader? Mark an X on each timeline below where you think the big event should go, to maximize the creative opportunities in your telling.

Afghan vet:

First page ⎯⎯⎯⎯⎯⎯⎯⎯⎯⎯⎯⎯⎯⎯⎯⎯⎯⎯⎯⟶ Last page

_____

_____

_____

_____

Olympic athlete:

First page ⎯⎯⎯⎯⎯⎯⎯⎯⎯⎯⎯⎯⎯⎯⎯⎯⎯⎯⎯⟶ Last page

_____

_____

_____

_____

Lottery winner:

First page ——————————————————————————→ Last page

_____

_____

_____

_____

Now, what comes before and after? If much of the length of your timeline is before the big event – as is probably the case with your athlete – what kind of events are going to build up to this? What kind of story is the bulk of the main narrative going to be? Jot your ideas down beneath each of the timelines.

The Afghanistan veteran's story should position the *X* somewhere around the middle of the timeline above. The narrative will naturally focus on the change war wrought on this individual, so it could fruitfully explore what drove this person to join up, and draw out the relationship between perhaps a need for comradeship before and during their time in Afghanistan, but a sense of abandonment afterward. Placing the tour of duty in Act 2 of a three-act story is the fecund creative choice.

The lottery winner's timeline could take two *X*s, I think: it could open with the big win, and all the craziness around it, then flashback to life before it was disrupted. Starting with the big event, then flashing back to how life was before the win, injects pace and intrigue into the movement where we get to know the Ordinary Joe protagonist.

Now, the final part of this exercise: Can you jot a value progression for each story? Use loyalty and betrayal as the core values for each story.

Afghan vet:

——————————————————→ Tour of duty ——————————————————→

_____

Olympic athlete:

————————————————→ Gold medal ————————————————→

Lottery winner:

————————————→ Jackpot ———————————→ Jackpot ————————→

The **combat vet** could feel betrayed by a poor tactical decision that left his buddies exposed. He could reach self-betrayal when he loses his joy of life, as he struggles with survivor guilt and maybe Post-Traumatic Stress Disorder. His story could end with a positive return to loyalty, as perhaps he prioritizes loyalty to self and loved-ones over loyalty to the corps.

The **Olympic athlete** could be betrayed by an injury that makes her miss her first Olympics. She could reach self-betrayal when painkiller dependence, or control issues in her eating, become a problem. A fight-back to loyalty to her trainers and supporters could presage a new state of loyalty to self, when her progression in life is rewarded with the ultimate professional accolade.

The **lottery winner** could hit betrayal, when the media circus moves from celebration to mean-minded persecution, and descend to self-betrayal soon after, when they feel forced to leave their old life behind and become the kind of rich person they hoped they'd never be. A wake-up call and a return to the values of their pre-jackpot life could permit a positive up ending for this life story, too.

In each of the examples above, I hope you found the ideas and perspectives that thinking in terms of core-value progressions brings helpful in getting to the heart of the material. Let's take a final look at how this writerly approach can help authors address even deeply sensitive, yet potentially emotionally resonant, life-writing material.

→ Case study: Core-value progressions in life writing

A particular group of life writers are active right now, creating an important contribution to social history. The last surviving Veterans of World War II are elderly men and women now, all with interesting stories to tell. Many may not have shared their memories before, not wishing to distress their families.

However, their grandchildren, and even great-grandchildren, are busy all over the world writing down their loved-one's memories for family posterity. It's an important project of social history, being undertaken individually by thousands of people across the Allied nations, now that even the youngest Veterans are in their nineties. For many of these life writers, it's the first big project they've attempted.

I've worked with a few such budding authors and almost always see a progression in their work on the theme of betrayal, however positive the story or heroic the experiences related. It follows a natural path of progression:

Outbreak of war: The protagonist is in a state of loyalty to self and loved-ones, striving to build career and future.

Split allegiance rears its head, in the thick of danger, when loyalty to comrades begins to outweigh thoughts of personal safety.

Betrayal comes when disaster strikes. Misguided orders from HQ send the protagonist into lethal danger, or a vital piece of kit fails on a warplane or ship.

↓

Feelings of **self-betrayal** come later, as the protagonist struggles with 'survivor guilt', or feeling they must keep part of themselves shut off from loved-ones now, lest the horrors of war spill out.

Naturally, few authors who sit down to record a beloved relative's wartime experiences would be thinking of the material in terms of betrayal. Such a negative word would be the last thing on their minds, which would naturally be full, instead, of heroism, courage and self-sacrifice. A negative term like 'betrayal' is at odds with the emotions they feel as they sit down to transform the collection of their loved-one's jokey anecdotes, and serious stories told *sotto voce*, into a narrative record for family posterity. But progressions on the core values of loyalty and betrayal may well emerge naturally in the deep narrative these stories tell.

But change the history a little and, of course, a different value emerges. A wartime career interrupted by capture might look like this:

When war breaks out, the protagonist is in a state of **fairness**, living among loved-ones, striving to build career and future.

↓

Unfairness enters the picture as the natural frustrations of war – of seeing comrades killed or loved-ones put at risk because the enemy has better equipment or tactics – develop for the protagonist.

↓

Tyranny, the extremity of the core-value progression, is experienced when disaster strikes, and the protagonist is captured. Even if treated well, the protagonist is deprived of almost all liberty – particularly the freedom to fight this enemy threat to their country, loved-ones and way of life.

↓

The complex value of **injustice** follows the armistice, as the protagonist struggles with 'survivor guilt', or with feeling that they must keep part of themselves shut off from loved-ones lest the horrors of war spill out.

Working with core-value progressions from the outset – from the planning stage of writing – helps an author build on the strengths of the story that they have to tell. The precision with which they choose what to include, what to foreground or efface, what moods to build as the story progresses, and how to order each movement of sequenced material is greatly enhanced when the driving forces of the narrative are mapped out from the start.

Where to next?

The basic creative building blocks of core-value progressions help novelists, dramatists and life writers bring their material to life on the page, deliver its core 'message', and make it resonate with readers. In the next chapter we'll work on the line-by-line nitty-gritty of creative writing, focusing on that most distilled and powerful of literary arts: poetry. From creating original imagery, to working with metaphors and subtext, we'll explore and practise the techniques poetic authors use to grab a reader's attention, and maybe even their emotions, with just a smattering of ink on a page.

Ideas and inspirations

▶ Creative life writing uses character arcs and plot progressions just like fiction and drama do.

▶ Life writers structure character and story development in their work to create coherence and resonance.

▶ Core-value progressions and character arcs can structure life writing and inject pace as powerfully as they do in fiction, poetry or drama.

▶ Technical thinking about character arcs and structural progressions helps authors distil the essence of life stories, and permit depth and meaning to emerge from surface complication.

8 Poetry: Bringing it together on the page

In this chapter you will learn:

▶ About imagery in creative writing, and how authors use it to bring depth and meaning to their work.

▶ How to construct similes, and use this building block of imagery to power creative concepts.

▶ How to create metaphors and deploy original authorial insights in the service of your creative project.

▶ How to turn your own perspectives and observations into powerful fuel for your work.

We've explored some of the deep structures that underpin creative writing; now let's look at what the reader sees – the words on the page – as we explore the most distilled and concentrated way to encode meaning and emotional power in words alone: poetry.

→ Creating imagery: Similes

Poets use imagery both to animate their writing and to involve a reader in its interpretation. Similes are a type of imagery, where one thing is compared to another, for illuminative effect: 'White as snow' or 'White like a fresh snowfall', for example.

Natasha Trethewy's poem 'Incident' is a work of great power and subtlety, which depends entirely upon two carefully chosen similes. It describes a terrible time in American history: the century leading up to the end of State-sanctioned apartheid.

The poet is not specific regarding the date; the incident she describes in the poem could have occurred at any time from the Civil War years to the last decades of the twentieth century. Neither does Trethewey tell us anything about the speaker in the poem, other than that she witnessed the incident of the title with her family years before. The power and depth of meaning of this remarkable poem rest entirely its two similes:

- ▶ 'a few men gathered, white as angels in their gowns'
- ▶ 'the cross trussed like a Christmas tree'

The narrator of the poem uses these similes to tell us about an incident years before, on the front lawn of her home. As she and her family peered terrified from behind drawn curtains, members of the Ku Klux Klan gathered on the grass out front, erected a cross, and burned it.

The poet transmits this information with just these two similes. An aberrant outrage is described using simple, everyday devices of speech: we all use similes, all the time. A simile compares one thing to another, typically using 'like' or 'as' to make the comparison: 'That wind's like ice.'

Everyday use of similes is typically jocular: 'Those cocktails last night were like rocket fuel'; 'My mouth tastes like the bottom of a birdcage.' We use them most often when we want to make light of a predicament: 'It's cold as a witch's teat out there.' The best similes require a little thought to interpret, to 'get', even if the 'getting' is simply the realization that fun is being made: 'The traffic was like the tenth circle of hell tonight.'

Trethewey uses the two similes in her poem similarly to involve us in what she's saying. Her particular focus on the Christmas tree and gowned angel similes – her narrator repeats them, yet holds back almost all other information – makes them stand out on the page.

So we're not told about the Ku Klux Klan, only of men 'white as angels in their gowns'. We're not shown a conflagration on the front lawn, only a 'cross trussed like a Christmas tree', garlanded with light. The terrible meaning of the poem, and the deep human empathy it evokes, rests on these two foregrounded similes.

Because we realize that, when this outrage occurred, these similes are how the bewildered parents described what was happening outside their home to their terrified children. Using the power of simile, the speaker's parents transformed a grave act of terrorism into a thing of beauty for their kids: men dressed as angels, a tree decorated with light. The deep human feelings this realization provokes in us augment the power of Trethewey's beautiful poem.

Exercise 40

WORKING WITH SIMILES

Wilfred Owen was a young British poet who fought and died on the front lines of World War I. His powerful verses, written direct from the combat zone, bring home all the inhuman horror of the time.

In his classic poem 'Dulce et Decorum Est', Owen uses similes to involve his reader viscerally in the awful realities of warfare. The poet's use of strong imagery, inviting us to make mental pictures of the scenes he's describing, allow us to share some of the nightmarish experience, even a century later. Can you list the similes Owen uses in the first stanza of this powerful poem?

> *Bent double, like old beggars under sacks,*
>
> *Knock-kneed, coughing like hags, we cursed through sludge,*
>
> *Till on the haunting flares we turned our backs,*
>
> *And towards our distant rest began to trudge.*
>
> *Men marched asleep. Many had lost their boots,*
>
> *But limped on, blood-shod. All went lame; all blind;*
>
> *Drunk with fatigue; deaf even to the hoots*
>
> *Of gas-shells dropping softly behind.*

_____

_____

_____

_____

_____

_____

_____

_____

_____

_____

Though every single line of this powerful verse is freighted with vivid imagery, there are only two similes, one in each of the opening two lines. But, as I'm sure you've noticed, there are many other images in this poem. See if you can pick them all out.

_____

_____

_____

_____

_____

_____

_____

_____

_____

Owen uses so many powerful images in this verse that they blend seamlessly with the narration. How many of the following did you manage to find?

- ▶ Bent double
- ▶ Haunting flares
- ▶ Marched asleep
- ▶ Blood-shod
- ▶ Drunk with fatigue
- ▶ Hoots of gas-shells
- ▶ Dropping softly

All of these images compare what's being described in the poem to something outside it, in order both to illustrate and make a point. The men aren't literally bent double, with their shoulders bumping their shins; the gas-shells aren't floating down like feathers. Owen describes the shells as 'dropping softly' to help us experience the horribly muffled way these particular missiles dispense death at point of contact. He describes the men as 'bent double' because they're carrying the burden of this global conflict on their exhausted shoulders.

Now, can you rewrite each of the images in the list above as similes? For example, the 'hoots of gas-shells', rewritten as a simile, could be 'the gas-shells hooted like owls'. Remember to use a comparison word, such as 'like' or 'as'.

_____

_____

_____

_____

_____

_____

_____

_____

_____

→ Creating imagery: Metaphor

The similes you created above were developed, by you, from Owen's original metaphors. You reverse-engineered them. As you probably discovered, as you created 'like' or 'as' comparisons, to turn Owen's metaphors into your own similes, a metaphor is simply a simile where the comparison is left out:

▶ A **simile** says that A is like B

▶ A **metaphor** says that A is B

Because his priority was impact and power, to tell a terrible truth that the world didn't want to know, Wilfred Owen needed high-impact imagery. So he used metaphor heavily, as well as simile, in his imagery, to close the gap between the reader and the experience described.

For example, instead of saying that the gas-shells hooted like hunting raptor predators as they fell, Owen prompts the image with the metaphor: 'hoots of gas-shells'. A simple powerful image prompts the imaginative connection, freighted with our inbuilt fear of predation – the very horror that Owen is reporting.

Similarly, instead of saying that the wounded soldiers look like they're wearing shoes made of blood, Owen says that they are 'blood-shod'. The simile that describes the image is weak, but the metaphor that distils it is powerful. 'Blood-shod' makes us feel the horror of limping through the mayhem of battle, boots squelching with your own leaking blood.

All but two of Owen's descriptive phrases, in the first stanza of 'Dulce Et Decorum Est', are metaphors:

▶ Bent double

▶ Haunting flares

▶ Marched asleep

▶ Blood-shod

▶ Drunk with fatigue

▶ Hoots of gas-shells

▶ Dropping softly

Owen uses two similes for fast scene-setting in his hit-the-ground-running first two lines, but otherwise deploys metaphors thick and fast throughout. Metaphors distil similes to a striking essence, making us conjure mental pictures as we interpret them: exactly the effect a soldier reporting difficult truths to folks back home from a hellish frontline needs.

So, instead of saying that the battle-flares shimmer in the sky like ghosts, Owen distils the simile to a metaphor: 'haunting flares'. Instead of saying that the soldiers are so tired that they're staggering around like booze hounds at chucking-out time, Owen boils the simile down to the metaphor: 'Drunk with fatigue'. We're invited to make the connection, to draw the picture – of soldiers staggering helplessly as exhausted limbs betray them – ourselves.

Similes and metaphors are powerful ways for all creative writers to engage their readers: to get them into the world of the piece and experiencing it. In poetry, their use is naturally paramount, particularly where the poet wishes – like Owen – to bring home a necessary truth to the reader.

Because, at the time Owen was writing, the British nation was yet to recognize the full horrors of what was happening in the trenches. Owen's reference in the title – to the Latin tag *Dulce et decorum est pro patria mori* [It is a sweet and fitting thing to die for one's country], typically inscribed on British war memorials – is used savagely in the last line of his poem, which condemns the phrase as 'the old lie'. Having been invited to share the horrors of the trenches, through Owen's strong use of powerful metaphors and similes throughout his poem, we are moved to concur with the poet's damning conclusion.

Exercise 41

WORKING WITH METAPHORS

Wilfred Owen's poetry reflects a strong journalistic duty to record his experiences, in order to bring home the horrors of what was actually happening in the war to a public still full of fervour. His strong use of metaphor in his short poem 'The Last Laugh' again immerses the reader powerfully in the frontline experience:

> 'O Jesus Christ! I'm hit,' he said; and died.
>
> Whether he vainly cursed, or prayed indeed,
>
> The Bullets chirped—In vain! vain! vain!
>
> Machine-guns chuckled,—Tut-tut! Tut-tut!
>
> And the Big Gun guffawed.
>
> Another sighed,—'O Mother, mother! Dad!'
>
> Then smiled, at nothing, childlike, being dead.
>
> And the lofty Shrapnel-cloud
>
> Leisurely gestured,—Fool!
>
> And the falling splinters tittered.
>
> 'My Love!' one moaned. Love-languid seemed his mood,
>
> Till, slowly lowered, his whole face kissed the mud.
>
> And the Bayonets' long teeth grinned;
>
> Rabbles of Shells hooted and groaned;
>
> And the Gas hissed.

The poet uses metaphors in almost every line of this poem, in order to drive home his central message. One of the particular horrors of World War I was that death was mechanized. Young men who'd barely seen a motor car or a corn-threshing engine were mown down by mechanized machine guns, flamethrowers, tanks and screaming artillery. Their daily experience was of industrialized slaughter.

Let's try identifying the metaphors Owen uses to animate 'The Last Laugh'. See if you can list them below:

1. _____

_____

2. _____

_____

3. _____

_____

4. _____

_____

5. _____

_____

6. _____

_____

7. _____

_____

8. _____

_____

9. _____

_____

The nightmarishness of missiles and mustard gas having the attributes of living things – bomb splinters 'tittering' as they rain down death, bullets chirping like birds or crickets as they fill the air – brings home the bewildered horror young men from a more peaceful era must have felt when faced with industrial murder-machines.

Wilfred Owen's genius in this poem is not just to describe the soldiers in human terms, but to describe mechanized death in the same way. The heart-breaking pathos of a young man's yearning for his sweetheart as he dies is witnessed by a derisive crowd, in Owen's poetic transformation:

→ Bayonets' long teeth grinned

→ Rabbles of shells hooted and groaned

→ Gas hissed

The imagery conjures a heckling, mocking mob as the only witness to the inhuman tragedy all around. Owen's other metaphors develop the effect:

→ Bullets chirped

→ Machine-guns chuckled

→ Big-guns guffawed

→ Shrapnel-cloud leisurely gestured

→ Falling splinters tittered

→ Face kissed the mud

It's natural to try to put a human face on an unknown quantity: 'the sun's trying to break through' is a much-uttered phrase on chilly British beaches in high season, for example. Owen 'spins' this human coping strategy – to humanize the unknown – with vivid metaphors in his poem, allowing us to glimpse the horror of mechanized death raining down all around, and the pathos of young men slaughtered in the mire, as if we were there.

Can you break down each of this poem's metaphors into its basic comparison? What are the big guns guffawing like, for example? Schoolchildren over a new haircut? Drunk uncles at Christmas?

1. _____

   _____

2. _____

   _____

3. _____

   _____

4. _____

   _____

5. _____

   _____

6. _____

   _____

7. _____

   _____

8. _____

   _____

9. _____

   _____

I hope that got your creativity flowing. Now let's look at the process of thinking up striking imagery to enhance and augment your work.

→ Creating original Imagery: A guided analysis

Whether you're a poet or a travel writer, a memoirist or an author trying their hand at fiction, crafting original and striking images to animate and illuminate your work is key to making your writing come alive on the page for a reader.

As you begin working with metaphors and similes, finding inspiration for original imagery of your own can begin to seem like chasing the rainbow. It's a tough skill to master, but it breaks down into basic approaches that anyone can take on.

For example, you're out for a stroll on a breezy day, and you see a dandelion clock giving up its pale little parachutes to the wind. Perhaps it's something you haven't noticed since childhood, when you used to pick ripe dandelions and blow away the feathery seeds yourself, but today it strikes you as amazing, and you decide to write about it. You set about trying to capture what you're seeing in an original and striking image.

So where do you begin? Your mind might be racing after similes and metaphors already – I've already been tempted, calling the windborne seeds 'parachutes' in the paragraph above. But let's put the brakes on and start by asking a more basic question.

WHAT IF?

The exact nature of the 'what if' questions you ask as you begin to create imagery is entirely open. The best way to approach this building block of original imagery is to think of as many 'what ifs' as you can. To return to our dandelion:

▶ What if the feathery seedlings blowing in the wind are actual dandelion parachutists?

▶ What if the feathery seedlings are sprites being born?

▶ What if the feathery seedlings are an artist's paint, fluffy traces documenting in the flaring yellows of new flowers the patterns of the wind through the seasons?

Concentrating on the seedlings alone, as the focus of a 'what if' question, can open all kinds of avenues to original imagery straight away. Using 'what if' questions that take the dandelion as a single entity creates similar opportunities:

▶ What if this dandelion was sentient? How would it feel as it releases its seed-voyagers into the wind?

- What if this dandelion wasn't a natural thing, but a self-replicating machine?
- What if the dandelion clock was an actual clock, to another species?

Taking the 'what if' question to the next level refines the imagery you're working with into the substance of story on the page. In the third example above, for example, a children's story vole with a busy day ahead could consult the dandelion clock to see if the morning winds have finished blowing. In the second example, the dandelion could contain a 'sleeper' code in its DNA, a blueprint of poisons that work on carbon-based species to clear our planet for alien invasion. In the first example, an image using a sentient dandelion could, perhaps, animate a creative piece about a parent's feelings as children leave home.

Exercise 42

WORKING WITH 'WHAT IF' QUESTIONS

Take a notebook out on a few observational forays – into town, into the countryside, to the hills or a riverbank or the seashore – wherever might stimulate you. You'll be amazed at how many striking things you spot when your only business is to look around with interest.

When something catches your eye, record it. As you do so, concentrate on experiencing the feeling that made you pick this out. Ask yourself the 'what if' question that that feeling prompts:

→ What if that gutter-perching bird has been blown off course by an ocean storm and is trying to get a handle on where it is?

→ What if that spent firework under the hedge had a prayer written on the shaft?

→ What if that hand-in-hand retired couple are professionals leaving the scene of a hit?

The nature of the 'what if' questions you ask will depend on your focus and sensibilities as a writer. The only important thing is to ask lots of them, as often as you can. Get into the habit, and you'll soon get used to creating and refining original imagery as second nature.

Schedule a few writing-time forays in the next few weeks if you can. For now, see if you can make ten 'what if' questions from what you see in the next 48 hours. If you don't have time to go out on a hunt in those 48 hours, all the better. See if you can create 'what if' questions with just what you encounter every day.

1. _____

_____

2. _____

_____

3. _____

_____

4. _____

_____

5. _____

_____

6. _____

_____

7. _____

_____

8. _____

_____

9. _____

_____

10. _____

_____

→ Metaphor and simile: Reader engagement

Using original imagery, metaphors and similes, and combinations of the two, is a sure-fire way to get a reader into the world of a piece and engaged with its perspectives. Emily Dickinson's much-loved poem about a mainline train begins:

> *I love to see it lap the miles*
> *And lick the valleys up*

The speaker of the poem is comparing the train to a prodigious animal, devouring the countryside as it powers across it.

But there's more going on here. The poet doesn't limit the metaphor by over-qualifying the image – saying the train is a speeding cheetah, or a very hungry caterpillar boring through the green country. Instead, Dickinson lets the reader enjoy the association sensually, feeling the power and speed of the train, as she does ('I love to see it…').

The poet has crafted her metaphors here to help us share the experience further. The precise detail of the images helps us adopt the perspective on the action which the poet will develop: the bird's-eye view of a train coursing through valleys and 'eating up the miles'. If we're watching an animal 'lapping' and 'licking up', we're probably looking down on it. To look down on a train as we'd look down on a dog, we have to adopt a fairly lofty vantage. So, with a brisk deployment of targeted metaphors in her first lines, Emily Dickinson takes her reader to the precise vantage-point – a helicopter shot, in modern TV terms – from which we can experience the power and speed of the train sensually.

The poem uses a basic pattern of set-up and pay-off to achieve the effect. The initial metaphors 'set up' the action and perspective of the poem – that the train moves like a powerful hungry animal – before the verses develop the comparison to pleasing effect – for example, when the train stops at a station, and its steam blast as it lurches back into action is compared to the roaring neigh of a mythical horse.

The 'Martian' poem by Craig Raine we worked with briefly in Chapter 4 uses a similar pattern of set-up and pay-off to achieve its effect. By making the familiar unfamiliar, viewing everyday life from the perspective of an extraterrestrial, the poem challenges us from its very first lines:

> *Caxtons are mechanical birds of many wings*
> *and some are treasured for their markings –*
> *they cause the eyes to melt*
> *or the body to shriek with pain.*
> *I have never seen one fly, but*
> *sometimes they perch on the hand.*

A reader new to the poem needs to work hard with this opening, suspending incomprehension as they try to work out what's going on. A riddle has been set by the poet, clearly, but he's given us a generous clue in the poem's title. This is an extraterrestrial describing earthly phenomena, we can see, even if we're not entirely sure what yet. We read on, tantalized by this set-up sequence – what 'mechanical' birds, 'treasured for their markings', could possibly 'cause the eyes to melt | or the body to shriek with pain'? Craig Raine's intriguing poem continues:

> *Mist is when the sky is tired of flight*
> *and rests its soft machine on the ground:*
> *then the world is dim and bookish*
> *like engravings under tissue paper.*
> *Rain is when the earth is television.*
> *It has the property of making colours darker.*

We're on firmer ground here, with the mystifying noun of the first movement – 'Caxtons' – replaced by 'Mist' and 'Rain' as the subjects of these sentences. This is a pay-off sequence, to reward us for reading on. It hints at how to solve the riddle and understand what this Martian is saying.

'Mist is when the sky is tired of flight' and 'Rain is when the earth is television' are metaphors we can interpret easily ourselves, and enjoy their striking and unusual perspectives. The first metaphor of this pay-off sequence uses two metaphors combined into one: the sky as a 'soft machine' that gets fatigued and has to rest, creating mist.

This compound metaphor is then developed with easily digestible similes, to make sure we 'get' the alien visitor's perspective:

▶ The first metaphor is 'When the sky is tired of flight'

▶ The second metaphor is 'rests its soft machine'.

The image-developing similes are 'bookish' and 'like engravings under tissue paper'.

So this pay-off sequence comes in two parts: an opening section (about mist) that uses metaphors and then similes, to help us understand how to 'read' this poem; and a concluding couplet to show us the perspective in the powerful and condensed form of metaphor – 'Rain is when the earth is television'.

 Exercise 43

USING METAPHORS FOR SET-UP AND PAY-OFF SEQUENCES

Craig Raine's 'A Martian Sends a Postcard Home' is a poem that uses sequences of set-ups and pay-offs to teach us how to 'read' and enjoy the unusual perspective it exploits. Here is its final sequence, which sets up the closing couplets:

> *Only the young are allowed to suffer*
> *openly. Adults go to a punishment room*
> *with water but nothing to eat.*
> *They lock the door and suffer the noises*
> *Alone. No one is exempt*
> *and everyone's pain has a different smell.*

The Martian has turned from talking about the weather to talking intimately about the inhabitants of this strange planet. But what mystifying process is he describing here? Can you break it down?

 What does the first of these couplets do, as you read it? What's its function in this set-up sequence?

_____

_____

_____

_____

_____

_____

_____

_____

_____

_____

The first couplet introduces the subject of this sequence: the mysterious adult human practice of visiting a 'punishment room', while the young 'suffer openly'.

It's a hook line, to get us into the set-up sequence and intrigued. What on earth is being described here?

The set-up sequence develops by offering a hint of a pay-off: the 'punishment room' is described in detail, in the second couplet. We're given some clues as to what the alien means.

This helps us interpret the final couplet, the internal pay-off to this sequence. We finally 'get' that the Martian is talking about bowel movements and bathrooms. But this is in itself a set-up sequence, taking us to the poem's final pay-off:

At night when all the colours die
they hide in pairs
and read about themselves –
in colour, with their eyes shut.

Metaphors stack up here, as the poet fires up all the burners for his grand final flourish – a lovely final couplet. Can you identify all the metaphors in this final sequence?

There are quite a few, delivered in just a few words, as the poet's rhythm shifts to brevity for closing impact. Darkness is conveyed by talking about colours dying; sleeping is 'hiding' two by two; dreaming is reading about oneself, internally, in colour.

The metaphor for dreaming – reading about oneself in colour – is itself a combination of metaphors that create a striking and unexpectedly moving closing image. It's a satisfying pay-off to an intriguing poem, which teaches us how to read and enjoy it by organizing its images into increasingly revelatory sequences of set-up and pay-off. (And if those 'Caxtons' of the first lines are still puzzling you, the many-winged birds with intricate markings... you're looking at one right now. William Caxton was the first English printer of books.)

→ Set-up and pay-off on the page: Subtext

Whether you're writing nuanced scenes for a novel, representations of real life for memoir or historical biography, or distilling human processes for poetry, creating patterns of set-up and pay-off in your work, using imagery freights your work with meaning and subtext.

Subtext is the deep meaning beneath the surface. Robert Browning's classic poem 'My Last Duchess' (which we looked at in Chapter 4) deploys subtext to intriguing yet ultimately chilling effect, as it escalates patterns of set-up and pay-off sequences. It begins:

> *That's my last Duchess painted on the wall*
> *Looking as if she were alive. I call*
> *That piece a wonder, now: Frà Pandolf's hands*
> *Worked busily a day, and there she stands.*
> *Will't please you sit and look at her?*

The speaker is a Renaissance duke entertaining a visitor – showing off his luxuries, it seems. Frà Pandolf is the name of a (fictitious) famous artist, and the Duke uses it to flatter his guest: he name-checked the artist deliberately, he goes on to say, because he knew his visitor would appreciate the subtleties of such a master's artistry in this portrait of his late wife.

The Duke's speech is all very courtly and polite through this set-up sequence of the poem, piling up flatteries and flowery phrases as he turns the visitor's attention to his point: the warm expression of intimacy captured on his wife's face by the artist. This is the first pay-off of the poem:

> *[...] Sir, 'twas not*
> *Her husband's presence only, called that spot*
> *Of joy into the Duchess' cheek [...]*

The Duke, we realize, isn't interested in enjoying the painter's artistry: his point is to complain about the Duchess. Not only is she gazing too intimately out from the portrait, even in death, for the Duke's taste; she was in life, it seems, too intimate with the rest of the world for him to stomach.

We get the feeling this duchess didn't die of natural causes. A short set-up sequence, describing how simple flattery from Frà Pandolf would have made the Duchess's eyes glow as in the portrait, suggests that she may have had a wandering eye. The pay-off which follows seems to confirm it:

> [...] *She had*
> *A heart – how shall I say? – too soon made glad,*
> *Too easily impressed; she liked where'er*
> *She looked on, and her looks went everywhere.*

Those last four words chill us through. We're reading about a lethal medieval form of domestic violence, it seems. The Duchess had a wandering eye; so the Duke took measures. Now she's the late Duchess; the implication that the Duke murdered her for adultery is very strong. This is the poem's subtext up to this point. But then the poem surprises us, almost exactly at its halfway point, delivering the true horror of what the Duke has done.

The Duchess didn't commit adultery at all: she displeased the Duke simply because she smiled as warmly at someone who picked blossoms for her, as at her noble husband. He found this behaviour incomprehensible:

> *She thanked men – good! but thanked*
> *Somehow – I know not how – as if she ranked*
> *My gift of a nine-hundred-years-old name*
> *With anybody's gift.*

This pay-off completes the absolute, polar-opposite turnaround of our sympathies which Browning achieves with his extraordinary poem. We began by seeing the Duke as a bereaved husband, a cultured man who remembers his wife warmly. The first set-up section brought us, however, to the first pay-off: the revelation that the Duke does not recall his wife as warmly as the opening lines suggested.

Another set-up section followed this, full once more of flowery language, but this time the pay-off was even more chilling: 'her looks went everywhere'. Abusive spouses throughout history and across class boundaries have cited a wandering eye, or overfamiliarity with people generally, as justification for their abusive actions. The Duke claims that his position in society justifies his attitude; but the sympathies evoked for his late wife, when the Duke describes her simple pleasures in life as if they were terrible insults to him, undercut his pompous claims as we read on.

The courtly language of the set-up sequences contrasts chillingly with the privileged bluntness of the rhetorical pay-offs, which the Duke builds to in his speech. For example, after exploring the idea that he could have talked to the Duchess about her unsatisfactory behaviour, instead of simply murdering her, he concludes that such discussion was not possible for him. To discuss where a spouse's behaviour falls short would for the Duke involve 'stooping', or descending from his lofty position to a human level:

> *[…] and I choose*
> *Never to stoop. Oh sir, she smiled, no doubt,*
> *Whene'er I passed her; but who passed without*
> *Much the same smile? This grew; I gave commands;*
> *Then all smiles stopped together.*

The sudden staccato effect created by the semicolons mark this as a final pay-off: the Duke admits that he had his wife killed. And he admits that he did it because she smiled too readily and naturally: she was murdered for enjoying life. Her basic humanity versus the Duke's inhumanity – his visitor, it turns out, is an envoy from the father of his potential next bride, and the Duke is issuing a warning – animate our emotions as we read this sequence of flowery set-ups and brutal pay-offs.

As the poem helps us interpret the Duke's metaphorical euphemisms – *stoop* means 'act like a human being', *I gave commands* means 'I ordered my wife's murder' – he transmutes, in our sympathies, from a cultured widower to a wealth-enabled monster. The subtext of the poem – the Duke's warning to his next bride, that she will be murdered if she fails to please – develops through tightly sequenced escalations of set-up and pay-off, and delivers a powerful message with its subtext: a damning indictment of socially mandated privilege and its abuses.

IMAGERY AND SUBTEXT

What's the hub of your neighbourhood? Everyone has one – a local shop, a street corner, a pub or coffee shop, a bench. Try to create a few similes that capture the essence, of the place or its people or both:

_____

_____

_____

_____

_____

_____

_____

_____

_____

_____

_____

_____

_____

Now turn your similes into metaphors: remember, a metaphor is just a simile with the stage of comparison (usually 'like' or 'as') distilled out.

_____

_____

_____

_____

_____

_____

_____

_____

Now reverse the sentiment behind of each of your images. If you just described a good thing, now make it bad – your friendly neighbourhood coffee shop could be an overbearing place full of the preening pretentious, for example. Similarly, if you began by describing a bad thing, now make it good – a sketchy street corner, with gang members striking menacing poses, could be the stage for an intricate yet minimalistic urban dance piece.

_____

_____

_____

_____

_____

_____

_____

As author, you are the god of subtext in your chosen world – the spin you put on something defines how your reader interprets and imagines it. Using imagery, and freighting it with subtext, is a powerful way to Show Don't Tell in your writing, involving your reader cerebrally, emotionally and sometimes even viscerally in your work as they read.

Where to next?

We've explored how poetry – a form that relies on economy and power – uses imagery to get a reader involved in the set-up and pay-off sequences of a creative piece. We've practised creating original imagery using the tried-and-tested creative technique of asking 'what if' questions, studied the use of subtext to add weight and power, and examined how powerful imagery animates set-up and pay-off dramatic sequences in creative writing.

Now we'll study a kind of writing that uses such dramatic sequencing to turn true-life events directly into compelling reading. From historical non-fiction like Dava Sobel's *Longitude,* to powerful reportage like Sebastian Junger's *The Perfect Storm*, we'll explore how non-fiction market-makers build on the writerly techniques we've explored, attracting massive readerships in this exciting growth sector of publishing.

Ideas and inspirations

- ▶ Metaphors and similes bring dimensionality to creative writing, engaging readers to experience the world of the work sensually and emotionally.

- ▶ Creating original imagery means exploring what the world has to offer, and asking 'what if' questions of what you find.

- ▶ Powerful subtext can be created with imagery and figurative language, deepening resonance and engagement.

- ▶ Poetry, in particular, can exploit developing sequences of metaphors and imagery, building meaning through progressing revelation.

9 Non-fiction

→ The non-fiction revolution

Just as poetry draws firmly on techniques of set-up and pay-off to achieve its effects, so creative non-fiction uses many of the techniques of storytelling to enthral its readership. Revolutions in journalism and literary writing, in the 1970s and 1980s, laid the foundations for a revitalized non-fiction sector whose stars – authors like Bill Bryson, Kate Summerscale and Sebastian Junger – now regularly supply mainline cash injections for the entire publishing industry.

Non-fiction authors have come to command large and lucrative readerships in recent decades, by utilizing techniques and ideas from both fiction and journalism. It's an exciting and fast-moving sector to work in, and the rewards can be spectacular – even for the unlikeliest works, such as Lynne Truss's surprise bestseller, *Eats, Shoots and Leaves*, about grammar and punctuation.

In today's creative non-fiction and travel writing, authors exploit many of the narrative principles we've explored already: principles such as Show Don't Tell, structural techniques such as core-value progressions, dramatic escalations such as sequences of set-up and pay-off. But though a mastery of such narrative tools is a necessary part of the modern non-fiction author's skill set, their chosen genre frees them to construct page-turning stories that draw on techniques from many modalities of writing – from poetry, journalism, even screenwriting and drama.

→ Non-fiction: Freeing the creative lines

Non-fiction can seem a more restricted place to work than other creative genres, in that a non-fiction author is bound to actual events. A biographer must stick to the verifiable facts of a life. A memoirist, though their subject is the entire breadth and depth of their own experience, mustn't venture beyond what actually happened – to second-guess the motives of someone from their past, for example, and represent them as actual on the page, would be libellous.

A travel writer must certainly stick to the facts of what they see and record, however tempting it might be to massage details to fit the story the author set out to write. The joy of this genre, in particular, is that the story one finishes with is usually very different from the initial expectation – in itself perhaps the essence of broadening horizons. The travel writer remains bound, however, to that which they actually experienced.

So where the poet or storyteller is free to invent, the non-fiction author can seem restricted at first glance. If there are points of stress in their material, or outright weaknesses they can't simply invent what they need to bridge the gap, as a storyteller would.

But this is where the revolution in non-fiction of the last few decades comes into play. Creative non-fiction authors aren't simply writing reports, or accounts of events, these days. They're creating fully fledged entertainment products designed to compete robustly in the marketplace for their full share of the leisure dollar, in an arena where even an amusingly written primer on punctuation can become a runaway bestseller.

→ Case study: Creative non-fiction in action

Let's study a non-fiction bestseller, familiar to many from its blockbusting Hollywood movie: Sebastian Junger's *The Perfect Storm*. This astonishing true tale of deep-ocean Armageddon has all the elements of a great novel:

▶ A poor fishing port on a harsh coastline, where the only option to build a life is to go to sea

▶ The pressures on this local industry, with foreign competition, declining stocks and escalating overheads forcing workers into ever-more dangerous waters

▶ The consequent imperative on local skippers to risk their crews, and those of rescue services, by fishing too far from winter landfall to run for shore when storms bare their teeth.

Hemingway would have enjoyed this material, and worked it into a powerful novel, but Sebastian Junger chose to present it to the world as non-fiction. His choice, far from restricting his options, greatly developed them.

Imagine a novel that might result from the factors bulleted above. The second point, for example, might force a novelist into a laborious subplot about quota meetings, or campaigning for protection from factory-fishing super-trawlers. A local-council firebrand, or a crusading journalist, would probably need to be invented, to deliver all the relevant information to the reader, and dramatize it in a dense subplot about vested interests and corruption. Such a novel might spend as much time on land as it does at sea.

But Junger's interest was in what the fishermen face, alone. He began research for the book as part of a magazine series on people with tough jobs – forest-fire fighters were another focus of the initial project. But, as Junger became aware of the straight economic correlation between the dangers North Atlantic fisherman face and their woeful injury and mortality rates, the author developed his material into a bestseller that won millions of readers.

The non-fiction form was for Junger a liberating choice. Instead of needing to invent multiple scene sequences, possibly even subplots, to convey the breadth of pressures on the fishermen, a non-fiction form meant Junger could simply deliver this information directly to the reader as part of his scene-setting. All of the detail a reader needs to know, if they're to understand the gravity of what's unfolding, can be delivered 'on the fly' in the non-fiction format Junger chose.

This freed Junger to devote all his page space to his real interest: the plight of under-the-cosh fishermen, and the coastguard daredevils who must attempt to rescue them, when there's nothing out there but thousands of miles of raging ocean.

TRUTH VERSUS FICTION: NARRATING EXTREME EXPERIENCES

For example, one of the vessels the narrative follows is a fishing boat that goes down with the loss of all hands in the big storm. The proximity of Junger's narrator to this crew – he's been there with them as they fought the weather for days and nights on end already – means he has to narrate their terrible fate in moment-by-moment detail. Junger's narrative approach demands that he doesn't skip out on his reader at this crucial moment, but continue his blow-by-blow narration to the terrible end.

This would be an awfully difficult scene to write as fiction. Most novelists would have to cut the narrative focus suddenly and dramatically, as the submerged vessel fills with water and the crew prepare for inescapable death – focusing instead, for example, on the last light bulb as it gutters. To stay with the crew as they die would be almost unbearable in fiction, and extremely difficult to write without descending into melodrama.

Yet Junger's chosen form, the non-fiction narrative, freed him to narrate this awful scene without betraying his blow-by-blow focus. He made the scene bearable by giving us the necessary information to understand it. Without dropping pace in his tight narration, Junger explains the 'dive reflex', and what happens physiologically when the human face is immersed in cold water; he discusses the sensations and physical processes of taking water into the lungs. As with most terrible situations in life, information mediates the horror of what's happening, and Junger's narrator is able to stay focused on the dying fisherman to the mortal end without a hint of prurience or poor taste.

Far from betraying his narrative project – to highlight the terrible pressures these coastal communities face in pursuing traditional livelihoods – Junger's form frees him to narrate even the very hardest of literary projects – death, even more difficult to write about than sex – in a way that millions of readers could be gripped by.

FREEDOM IN NON-FICTION

The non-fiction form, freed of the perennial fictional problem of 'exposition' – i.e., feeding a reader need-to-know information, so they may follow the action – can draw on all the strategies of journalism in an information-dense age to fuel its narrative purpose.

But that's not to say that a 2,000-word article or a long blog piece can simply be stretched out and written up into a 70,000-word book. The non-fiction author develops techniques from all genres of writing, including fiction and drama, to hone their narrative edge.

Let's focus in on the basic building blocks of *The Perfect Storm*'s story:

1. **Establishing the scene:** a rough-and-tough fishing port where economic pressures force skippers to fish dangerously close to the winter storm season

2. **Introducing the characters:** a respected local skipper having a run of 'bad luck' – the economic pressures in action – and his hard-bitten crew

3. **Introducing the milieu** – the pressures of the here and now that light the fuse on the action: it's the end of fishing season, now that the winter storms have begun to blow, but this skipper and his crew need to make one last score to stay afloat.

This story permits a straightforward set-up sequence, where the scene is set, the characters are introduced, and the milieu – the tail end of a tough season in a harsh business – provides the trigger for the story.

Can you dramatize this set-up sequence as fiction? Take each of the three points, numbered above, and try to think of the characters you would need and the kinds of scenes and sequences that might be involved, to achieve all three of the set-up processes described above:

1. _____

_____

_____

_____

_____

_____

_____

_____

_____

_____

_____

2. _____

_____

_____

_____

_____

_____

_____

_____

_____

3. _____

It's a fair amount, isn't it? And to deliver this all in literary storytelling mode might be a lengthy process for both author and reader. In Junger's approach, however, all of the necessary information regarding the above – much of it eye-opening and fascinating in itself – is delivered in journalistic prologues and interludes punctuating action sequences and reportage from rescue personnel and other storm survivors. This 'on the fly' approach to exposition means the story can escalate with inexorability and power, in lockstep with the inexorability and power of the perfect storm building at sea.

→ Case study: Structuring non-fiction

As we've just explored, fast-moving non-fiction that seems freed from the conventions of fictional storytelling can nevertheless exploit traditional dramatic structure – with set-up and pay-off sequences used to keep readers turning pages. For this case study, we'll use Dava Sobel's phenomenally successful *Longitude*.

ACT 1: OPENING SEQUENCE

Chapter 1 of *Longitude* maps the terrain, introducing the age-old, deadly serious problem of finding accurate positions for ships at sea. It introduces us to the various methods available to a pre-technological era, and helps us understand how solving this problem was a crucial factor in facilitating trade between nations, and progress toward modern civilization.

It also introduces the hero, John Harrison, and sketches how his astonishing voyage-proof clocks solved the problem – a feat made even more astonishing in that Harrison was a self-taught carpenter by trade, and bested the finest scientific minds of his day in finally making navigation at sea an accurate science.

It's a short chapter, packed with tightly narrated information. But it's also a pacey, intriguing read, with the weight of facts greatly mediated by Sobel's free-ranging narrative, which moves from personal experience and the present day (the wire-ball toy discussed in Chapter 3 of this book) to sketch out more or less the entire story the author has to tell.

It ends by relating how the hero was largely deprived of reward and recognition, for the decades of extraordinary work dedicated to his inventions, by gentleman scientists unwilling to concede that a mere carpenter could have solved the thorniest problem of their age. The theme of the narrative – its core value – is therefore also introduced here: this is to be a story about injustice.

Sobel can give away her entire story in the first chapter, including its denouement, because, although this is essentially a biography of Harrison and his achievements, her approach is that of the modern non-fiction author. Her confident use of narrative structure, paragraph by paragraph and chapter by chapter, allows her to make bold 'cuts' from sub-sequence to sub-sequence, creating a narrative that visits and revisits its material, building context and depth each time.

In Chapter 2, having now mapped the terrain of the book, Sobel begins these bold cuts, opening the chapter on board a British ship in 1707, about to run aground in fog with the loss of all hands – a longitude error is to blame. From an opening chapter narrative vantage-point, which surveyed the entire terrain of the book's project, Sobel zooms in to a very specific here and now. After a thrilling narration of the shipwreck, she pulls back again to recount the cost – human and economic – of longitude errors to shipping in Harrison's time.

So, having let us experience what was at stake in this matter emotionally, with her thrilling yet fearful tale of the shipwreck, Sobel allows us to appreciate the longitude problem's cost to humankind in general with some well-chosen illustrative facts. We've experienced the book's project emotionally and intellectually now, and the foundations of the tale are well laid. It's time for Act 1's first big dramatic crescendo.

ACT 1: MID-ACT CLIMAX

After her explanation of the longitude problem's cost to global trade in the decades immediately before the Industrial Revolution, Sobel zooms in again to another very specific here and now – another ship, another longitude error, another big death-toll disaster.

It's a gripping yet terrible true-life tale, narrated as dramatically and pacily as the first, but there are two big surprises – two big twists – here. The first is that the ship involved had just carried Harrison's invention on its first test voyage, where it had performed excellently. If it had still been carrying the clock – instead of Harrison's invention sitting under a dustsheet while the leading scientists of the day wrangled – its skipper would not have mistaken its position, and 250 or so lives would have been saved.

The second twist is that there's no shipwreck in this disaster: the terrible death toll this time is from scurvy, after a longitude error adds critical weeks to a voyage. The terrible gravity of the situation, and of the problem the humble carpenter Harrison set out to solve, is restated and reinforced by powerful twists at the mid-act climax.

⏱ Exercise 46

CREATING TWISTS

Twists are what sell movies and popular entertainment. Who doesn't love the twist at the end of *The Usual Suspects*, where Kevin Spacey's character stops limping, or the twist in *Star Wars* where Vader reveals his identity? All the best popcorn-fodder is stuffed with good twists.

Twists are essentially reversals of expectation. An author leads a reader's expectations in a certain direction, then surprises them. In *The Silence of the Lambs*, Hannibal the Cannibal turns out to be a cultured and brilliant man. In *Reservoir Dogs*, the gut-shot robber – whose loyalty none will question as he lays dying – turns out to be an undercover cop. Good twists reward audiences and readers alike, and are strongly respected.

Let's try creating a few of these inspirational moments. Consider each of the following scenarios:

1. A police chief is a pillar of the community, giving his spare time to teach English to new immigrants and mentoring troubled teens

2. A Victorian-era doctor is both greatly valued by clients for his prescriptions and a widely respected sexologist whose ideas reflect the morality of the age

3. An investment banker is a greedy so-and-so who uses women like he uses other people's money – he hits a new low when he seduces a young anti-capitalist protestor camped outside his office.

 Now twist your scenario. Clues as to where to go with the twists are in the detail I've provided.

1. _____

_____

_____

_____

_____

_____

_____

_____

_____

_____

_____

_____

_____

_____

2. _____

_____

_____

_____

_____

_____

3. _____

Twists look complex, often dazzlingly so, but in writerly terms they're simply set-ups and pay-offs. Each of the above scenarios has the set-up of a story-driving twist built in, which you probably exploited as you built your three twists.

The obvious twist with the cop is that he's corrupt. His leisure-time activities connect him with both a supply and a retail structure for a drugs business. Many mysteries and thrillers work this twist as a central or complicating factor in their plots, reflecting the time-honoured way in which prohibition encourages criminality.

The Victorian doctor is a pillar of rectitude who, in line with the practice of his era, prescribes heroin, cocaine and tincture of cannabis to his idle-rich clients, while strapping their sons into electrical anti-masturbation devices and pleasuring their wives with 'anti-hysteria' vibrators. Novels like T. C. Boyle's *The Road to Wellville* and *Riven Rock* fuel powerful stories with this entertaining twist on the private physician's role.

The banker's story is the scenario most ripe for the theme of redemption. Seducing an anti-capitalist protestor would be seen by such a man's colleagues as akin to bestiality, a 'new low' indeed. But the connection across otherwise insuperable class boundaries opens up a story that can build human values in the protagonist from scratch.

When readers and audiences rave about great twists, they're talking about pay-offs. To creative writers, twists are all about set-up: the process of building the equation that drives the pay-off into a narrative. Let's return to how Dava Sobel builds her intricately set-up narrative toward pay-off.

ACT 1: CLOSING PROGRESSION

The double-punch twists of Sobel's first mid-act climax – the death toll from scurvy and details of its terrible terminal effect are just some among the eye-openers here – make us read on eagerly, as the big dramatic twists of the mid-act climax signal to us that we're heading for the first big pay-off.

So it proves. Chapter 3 fleshes out the history of navigation, from the ancient world to the 'present day' of the narrative – Harrison's time. It covers the contributions of major figures such as Galileo and Cassini and the founding of the Royal Observatory at Greenwich specifically to study the problem of longitude. Like the very first chapter, this is a set-up sequence that, by giving us the history of the problem, reinforces the brilliance of its solution.

Sobel needs to return to Harrison's story in more depth now, so the set-up of Chapter 3 prepares us for the depth of detail we'll need to absorb now if we're fully to understand the importance of Harrison's achievement. A skilled tactician like Sobel pays off this detail by delivering it with the big emotional pay-off of the act climax.

ACT 1: CLIMAX

Sobel's fourth chapter is short and punchy, building and delivering the Act 1 climax. Having explored the longitude problem through history, and the various lines of inquiry pursued by thinkers, mathematicians and astronomers across the centuries, the author focuses now on what would become the lasting solution to the problem: Harrison's voyage-proof clock, accurate in tropical swelter as in Arctic gale, a feat of engineering considered impossible at the time – metals expand in heat and shrink in cold, critically affecting the accuracy of eighteenth-century timepieces.

It's this very impossibility which is the Act 1 climax. Sobel skilfully creates an 'all is lost' moment, where Harrison's task seems impossible, suggesting that for all his decades of work he would be bested by a rival approach to solving the problem. In traditional storytelling, as seen in most Hollywood movies (think of a romcom, for example), the 'all is lost' moment is the Act 2 climax, setting up the big twists of the third act. It's the moment where the 'quest' of the story appears doomed – only for the final act to turn things around, usually with a bittersweet kicker.

But Sobel's huge innovation as a non-fiction author, like Sebastian Junger and working at exactly the same time, was to apply the techniques of fiction in new ways to non-fiction. She located the 'all is lost' moment in the Act 1 climax, and for sound writerly reasons. Principle among these is that Sobel was here trialling a new approach to biography. Rather than writing an earnest biography of Harrison – one that begins with his death, before flashing back to his humble childhood and the struggles of his life – Sobel tells us Harrison's story three times in a circular narrative.

First, she sketches in the need-to-know stuff, in Chapter 1, outlining the inventor's entire life and death. Everything is up front: the humble beginnings; the achievement; the struggle with official scientists jealous of a carpenter encroaching on their patch; Harrison's exhausted and frustrated old age – it's all here. Every one of the 'cherries' with which a biographer would carefully stud their entire project is given away in a few cursory paragraphs at the end of the first chapter.

It's a bold approach – and to a traditional biographer, writing thoughtful chronological accounts, professional suicide – but Sobel is a talented author taking risks in her work. In her first chapter, she gives us the story in a nutshell, so that we can absorb detail and nuance freely as we read on, our interest piqued.

This frees Sobel to use a circular narrative design – we revisit Harrison's story again and again, with more context each time we focus back in on the detail of the hero's story. It's an approach that freights the material with depth – building a sketch of the man, then giving context and background, then building the biography some more. This visiting and revisiting of the material builds our understanding rather than 'blinding with science', allowing any reader to appreciate the extent of achievement described in Harrison's remarkable story.

ACT 2: FIRST SEQUENCE

So at the start of Act 2, Sobel's focus pulls out again, to discuss the contending solutions to the longitude problem, as pursued by Harrison's gentleman rivals. Again, this set-up sequence fleshes out the world of the story, giving us nuanced information about its 'quest' in its detailing of rival approaches. Chapter 5 culminates with the catalyst, the trigger for action: shipping interests in London petition the King to offer a spectacular cash prize to whoever solves the longitude problem, and the money is put up for grabs.

It's a powerful way back into Harrison's story, as Sobel continues to exploit the circular narrative technique. (We'll break this strategy down in detail when we look at Sobel's closing scenes.) This time, as we read of Harrison's struggles, we have a full picture of what's at stake: the cost to humanity, to economic progress – and a sensational jackpot for the scientist able to win the support of his fellows in favour of his own solution. As we return to Harrison's story, our appreciation of the threat to this hardworking genius from Establishment scientists with questionable motives is sharpened.

ACT 2: MID-ACT CLIMAX

Sobel is gingering us with this mid-sequence climax, before moving briskly to the mid-act climax. Now Harrison's story takes on new depth for us, as we read about the context of the longitude prize-pot and the great men involved, focusing on Sir Isaac Newton, discoverer of gravity. Appointed to head the Board of Longitude set up to solve the problem and pay out the King's cash jackpot, Newton dies after seven years' work. Chapter 6 concludes by telling us that even after Newton's death, it would be 40 more years before the prize money was paid.

This end-of-chapter pay-off slingshots us forward into a more detailed biography of Harrison than the first chapter's thumbnail sketch provided. It does so because it's another big twist:

> *[Newton] did not live to see the great longitude prize awarded at last, four decades later, to the self-educated maker of an over-sized pocket watch.*

We already know Harrison's dates, so understand that these 'four decades' mean that he'll be an old, old man before properly recompensed for his remarkable work. We also understand that this will almost certainly be down to Harrison's gentleman rivals, and their inability to stand the fact that a self-educated working man could out-think and out-engineer them. As in the first act, the second mid-act climax is delivered with a neat twist, deepening our engagement with the story.

ACT 2: SECOND SEQUENCE

We settle into the final half of this pacey second act with our interest piqued as to how Harrison's seminal inventions could have been thwarted for four decades, while shipping continued to be decimated all the while.

After the big surprises supplied by a more detailed biography of the inventor – absorbing technical achievements that surprise and intrigue us – this final sequence sets up the act climax by exploring the pressures Harrison's inventions faced from a coterie of established scientists with their own ideas as to where the jackpot prize should go.

ACT 2: ACT CLIMAX

In response, we learn that Harrison was self-effacing in the extreme – when exhibiting his clocks to the prize-giving board, he repeatedly spoke only of their defects and asked only for some baseline funding to continue his work.

The core value of this story is one of unfairness escalating to injustice, as Harrison is blocked again, and lives continue to be lost at sea. The end of the line will, of course, be tyranny, as Harrison's rivals change the goalposts and issue laws and edicts to thwart him, but the hero's character arc is important in this story, too.

Harrison reacts to escalating unfairness in this story with courage. He persists with his difficult and important work because he knows it's vital. But here his opening position of courage is developed. Now Harrison's mettle is recast as being both positive *and* negative by this bold act climax development.

It's a huge turnaround, and a big progression on Harrison's character arc. Up to now, we've seen Harrison's courage only positively. This humbly-born carpenter carved his first clocks from wood while barely out of his teens, though how he learned horology remains anyone's guess – there were no clockmakers within hundreds of miles of his tiny rural village, and no wealthy patrons with libraries at the young carpenter's disposal. Harrison's hardworking genius has been purely positive in the story so far.

But now the positivity of hardworking genius begins to be coloured by the negative overtones of perfectionism. History is filled with also-rans who focused in too closely to see the big picture, and we fear this may be Harrison's fate. The intellectual energy that spurred him to remarkable achievements so early in life could, we realize, make him expend the bulk of it on a largely thankless task. We're emotionally involved with this story from way back, thanks to Sobel's telling of the tale, and we don't want to see this fate befall the hero – we read on, as again Sobel's circular narrative pulls back the focus one last time for the start of her final act.

Exercise 47

RECASTING CHARACTER VALUES

Dava Sobel spins Harrison's courage and persistence with overtones of perfectionism, as the decades pass. The positive value of courage in Harrison's character arc begins to be coloured with potential negativity, building intrigue and anticipation into the story.

It's a powerful twist, to recast a strongly positive trait to such end, and Harrison's character arc takes a surprising and intriguing new direction. Recasting character values is a powerful tool that is exploited by authors across the creative spectrum.

Let's try it now. In Thomas Harris global bestseller *The Silence of the Lambs*, one of the most memorable villains in history pits his wits against a naive, rookie Federal Agent. But in doing so, he psychoanalyses her and frees her from the childhood traumas whose effects have coloured her life. Lecter does what Starling asks him to do: helps her find the strength and stability to take down the psychotic serial killer whose crimes drive the novel.

It's a story with a strong core-value progression. But every point on the progression is 'spun', by being recast with the opposite value one would expect.

Starling begins the novel as a trainee agent, living and breathing the FBI, wedded to its corporate culture and trendy ideas of criminal profiling. What's the core value here?

_____

Well done if you guessed loyalty straight away. Starling is a new recruit who is utterly loyal to her unit.

Then she meets Lecter, and he confounds her. He's a crazy serial killer, a guy who doesn't just turn living flesh into dead meat, but cooks his victims up and washes them down with fine wine. In terms of criminality, it's difficult to get more way-out than that.

But Lecter comes across immediately as a cultured and brilliant man, and immediately Starling's world starts to crumble. Her trendy theories say that serial killers give away their criminality in everything they do. But Lecter is only insightful, cultured and witty – if occasionally chillingly so. As their relationship deepens, he proves extraordinarily able and helpful. What does this process do to Starling's opening loyalty?

_____

Loyalty, a positive human value, is usually complicated in a narrative by split allegiance, and that's what happens here.

Split allegiance is usually a terrible place to be in life. No one likes to be caught between two stools, serving two masters, needing to wear two faces. But in Harris's mega-selling story, it's a good, positive development.

Starling's unthinking loyalty to the corporate culture of the FBI is undermined by things out in the real world: Lecter, primarily, a true man of the world. Starling's worldview and sense of self consequently begin the process of moving from immaturity to maturity. Just as Dava Sobel recasts positive hardworking courage with overtones of perfectionism, so Thomas Harris recasts a positive trait to create an intriguing twist to his acclaimed story.

He follows through, too, spinning the final two possible progressions on the arc just as strongly – Starling exercises self-betrayal when she gives up her most-guarded secrets to Lecter, and betrays her boss at the end of the book when she fails to turn in a postcard from the fugitive doctor. But both of these 'negative' developments, betrayal and self-betrayal, are huge positives in Clarice Starling's story, as she grows in maturity and catches the killer.

ACT 3: FIRST SEQUENCE

But Sobel isn't just making bold moves with her core values; she's using the powerful technique of circular narrative, as we've touched on already, to bring depth and meaning to her building story.

A **linear narrative** sets out the story chronologically. A biography of a great author, for example, will typically start with an illustrative event from the author's life, then flash back in time to tell how their parents grew up, met and married, before covering the author's birth, childhood, education and career chronologically.

A **circular narrative** uses chronology as a tool, not a rule. So having built her story to two act climaxes, Sobel pulls the focus back again, returning in her circular narrative to flesh out the detail of Harrison's rivals' efforts.

Their approach to determining longitude rested on observing the Moon's distance from certain stars, a terribly difficult metric to use. To begin, the Moon doesn't follow a regular path through the night sky, and over time it appears to speed up (an effect actually due to the spin of the Earth slowing down, braked by tidal friction). Many decades of astronomical observations were required, from all around the world, to even begin to tackle the problem. Yet teams of royally appointed mathematicians and astronomers toiled away for decades at this rival approach, while Harrison worked alone in his workshop, refining and perfecting the engineering of his clocks. We gain a new appreciation for how lonely Harrison must have felt, and the self-belief he must have had to muster.

The pay-off to this sequence, itself setting up the final mid-act climax, is to return for the last time to the detail of Harrison's story: this circular narrative's closing movement. Having a mastery of all the context and background information, now Sobel shows us the fine detail of Harrison's extraordinary engineering. Described almost as objects of art, the clockmaker's inventions shine out from the page, progressing in sophistication and complexity from large machines to the mid-act climax: a chronometer barely larger than a pocket watch.

ACT 3: MID-ACT CLIMAX

It's an astonishing development. By holding back a lush description of Harrison's inventions to the very last act, the revelation that – although the inventor's first three models were big, heavy pieces of kit – his fourth was a pocket watch makes our jaws drop. We've appreciated all the technical problems Harrison faced in devising his first prototypes, and assumed that big chunky devices would be required to overcome the seemingly impossible challenges faced.

So, to suddenly learn that Harrison's final prototype was the equivalent of shrinking a 1980s big-box computer to today's laptop is a real 'Wow!' moment. Finally, we appreciate the true depth of Harrison's achievement: after such an invention, surely he must have been lauded.

This final mid-act climax must serve a dual function: it must both pay-off what's come before and slingshot us powerfully into the final movement of the book. Here, Sobel's revelation pays off and slingshots beautifully: with such an invention as his pocket-watch chronometer, Harrison's wisdom must finally have prevailed.

ACT 3: FINAL SEQUENCE

But of course it didn't. Sobel's next chapter opens:

> *A story that hails a hero must also hiss at a villain – in this case, the Reverend Nevil Maskelyne, remembered by history as 'the seaman's astronomer'.*

The final sequence kicks off with a big twist – this acclaimed man is described as 'a villain'. The wellspring of intrigue is primed one final time, and we read on keenly.

Finally, we learn of the actual obstacles put in Harrison's way by the scientific committees appointed to find an accurate method of measuring longitude. Each of Harrison's successive inventions were sent on sea voyages and tested, where they performed excellently, only for the committee to change the trial's goalposts. Eventually, Harrison was being specifically named in official legislation regarding the search for longitude as someone whose methods were suspect. The self-deprecating, perfectionistic Harrison responded to each blow – like the doomed horse in Orwell's *Animal Farm* – by resolving to do better.

We learn of Harrison's son, his assistant for the decades he toiled on his final invention, the pocket-watch chronometer. We appreciate, with new depth, what drove Harrison to both invent a machine that could do the impossible, and then to reduce it in size by a factor of a pig bred for bacon to a hedgehog. The core-value progression and character arc are progressed again, as we appreciate anew the scale of Harrison's perfectionist achievement.

Harrison's character arc has moved from courage, unequivocally positive, to a kind of driven courage – perfectionism – that can be unhelpful and unhealthy. Harrison seems his own worst enemy, as he responds to injustice and insult by simply promising to do better. The central emotional hook of the story – that such a hardworking and brilliant man could be discriminated against throughout life because of his lowly birth, when so much was at stake – is powered home by developing both the character arc and the core-value progression here.

The key action of this final sequence is a humiliating test visited on Harrison by the scientific authorities. Over the course of a full week they made him disassemble his pocket chronometer and explain the construction and function of every component, while those present took detailed notes. He was then made to reassemble it without reference to notes or diagrams, surrender it to the Admiralty for ever, and build two replicas for further testing while his blueprints were published on the open market. In effect, Harrison was forced to give up all rights to his invention and treated like the prime suspect for a serious crime while he did so. The final *coup de grâce* was the confiscation, by official decree, of his first three prototypes.

ACT 3: STORY CLIMAX

Harrison's entire life's work had now been physically taken from him by rival astronomers and mathematicians who'd spent their own lives pursuing a different and inaccurate approach to solving the longitude problem.

Now came the final test: a voyage by none less than Captain James Cook, where the two rival methods would go head to head. On board were both a full set of lunar-measuring equipment, and a copy of Harrison's pocket watch. Even this final, prestigious trial was rigged: Harrison was not permitted to make the test chronometer himself.

Yet Cook returned full of delighted praise for the invention. Meanwhile, Harrison had built the replicas demanded of him, which the King himself supervised in trial (during which, once a cache of magnetic ore had been removed from an adjoining cellar, the watch performed excellently). However, a new Longitude Act of Parliament was pushed through by Harrison's rivals, specifying that no solution to the problem would become adopted until they'd tested it according to their own methods and handling for an open-ended period of years. Harrison was in his seventies at this point: plainly no recompense or recognition would be his. The Royal Astronomer, Nevil Maskelyne, was quoted as saying, basically, that this would show those plebs who was boss.

The story climax is, of course, Harrison's death, unrecognized and unrecompensed for his vital life's work, but esteemed and bestowed with, in Sobel's words, 'martyr status amongst clockmakers'. His invention, copied by contemporaries, continued to be tested by Maskelyne, who managed to actually break the primary test model with his handling of it. Yet successive clockmakers persisted, and ultimately one found a way to manufacture Harrison's chronometer cheaply enough for it to become the standard method for finding longitude at sea, thereby saving countless lives.

Exercise 48

STRUCTURING ON THE PAGE

Dava Sobel's *Longitude* uses a circular narrative within a three-act structure to achieve a four-part progression on its core value: justice. In Sobel's book, the value progression runs like this:

JUSTICE

Harrison is a talented young carpenter who teaches himself to carve working clocks. He is paid well to make them and realizes that his inventions and innovations could solve the biggest problem of the day: how to stop losing ships and crews at sea.

UNFAIRNESS

Despite his diligent and brilliant achievement, the working-class Harrison is discriminated against by upper-class Establishment figures who are pursuing the prize money themselves.

INJUSTICE

When Harrison's models perform excellently in long sea voyages, his rivals change the goalposts after the event and declare the tests invalid.

TYRANNY

Harrison's rivals actually change the law to discriminate against him, and force him to give up all the secrets of his inventions, and all rights to them. Harrison dies.

JUSTICE

Harrison's fellow clockmakers replicate and refine his inventions until they become standard in shipping, saving countless lives and vessels.

You'll notice, of course, that the final justice is only justice of a kind: Harrison died a disappointed man, despite receiving a medal from the King himself, who had the inventor's chronometer tested in the palace cellars at one point. He must have felt that he'd pulled his son, his assistant already for decades on end, into an impossible struggle with vested interests: a David and Goliath battle that he couldn't hope to win. It's a terrible way for a father to die, feeling he has condemned his son.

The justice that his fellow clockmakers finally secured for Harrison's invention is a bittersweet justice – verging on the bitter-sour. All the best stories, as I'm sure you'll agree, mix it up with their endings: humanity and human experience are complex. As Oscar Wilde once said, in art as in life 'the good rarely end happily, or the bad unhappily'.

Let's try working with a four-part value progression and a three-act structure – the same narrative techniques and tools Sobel used in her market-making bestseller. Pick a hero or heroine of yours – a present-day or historical figure about whom you know the whole nine yards. Someone whose life you admire and are intimate with.

What's the theme of this life story? What's its 'message'? What's the core value here? Jot down some ideas here:

_____

_____

_____

_____

_____

_____

_____

_____

_____

_____

_____

_____

_____

_____

_____

_____

_____

_____

_____

_____

_____

_____

_____

It's an interesting exercise to try to find something specific at the heart of a life story – but we all know that people's lives are meaningful in their own way. The old writer's adage that everyone has a story to tell, if you know how to listen, is very true.

So some core values that you might have located in your chosen values could be:

- ▶ **JUSTICE,** if your hero is someone like Martin Luther King or a heroine like Rosa Parks
- ▶ **COURAGE,** if you picked an achiever in a harsh field – this could be the core value in the story of Beyoncé, or Amy Winehouse with a different trajectory
- ▶ **GREED,** if you picked the story of someone who developed an unhealthy appetite, then had to work their way back from Insatiability to healthy satiety
- ▶ **LOYALTY,** if the life story you picked is one of betrayal, and possibly ultimately self-betrayal.

Now, can you identify the progression on that core-value in your chosen life story? Sketch some thoughts here:

_____

_____

_____

_____

_____

_____

_____

_____

_____

_____

_____

_____

_____

_____

_____

_____

_____

_____

If you're working with a **greed story,** it probably begins with satiety twisted by events into an Insatiable hunger. The normal human state of day-to-day satiety can only then be re-achieved with extraordinary effort and personal change.

In a **courage story,** such as that of a woman in a male-dominated arena like show business, the trajectory may shine out from your chosen life: the courage to enter the arena, the fear of failure, with pressures building to make your heroine reach the stage of 'fear pretending to be courage', and all the terrible life consequences that can have.

A **loyalty story** will also often start with the core value charged positively, before betrayal can often escalate – like 'fear pretending to be courage' – into all kinds of self-betrayal. A successful actor, for example, might sacrifice, in coping with the demands of career, the family life he set out to provide for.

Now see if you can break your chosen life story up into three acts. Having thought about your material thus far, it might break down quite easily for you. If you're stuck, go back to the analysis of *Longitude* above and briefly note down how each sequence and climax progresses the story – then use these notes to think about your chosen material here:

_____

_____

_____

_____

_____

_____

_____

_____

_____

_____

_____

_____

_____

_____

_____

_____

_____

_____

_____

_____

It may be that you were able to accomplish the above quite readily, or it may be that it took a lot of work. If you struggled, try again with an 'easier' figure, someone whose life is a little less complex and with a trajectory for good or ill clearly defined – try Janis Joplin or Kurt Cobain, if you're a rock fan, or Whitney Houston or Lance Armstrong if their lives are more familiar.

Either way, I hope you found that the three-act structure (with three mid-act climaxes and three act climaxes) is a surprisingly amenable tool to use when designing an account of a life story. The basic human progression of youth, maturity and old age maps naturally on to the three-part progression that a lifetime's experience of three-act novels, sitcoms and movies has prepared us for.

So, just as the novelist and screenwriter use three-act structure as their basic model, so creative non-fiction authors from biographers to self-help specialists exploit this standard structural technique to permit the deployment – as with Sobel's circular narrative and powerful character arc – of different strategies of involving and enjoyable writing.

Where to next?

We've explored how creative writers working in every genre use the same craftsman-like techniques and ideas to approach their craft:

1 Structural ideas such as core-value progressions and character arcs

2 Figurative devices, such as metaphors and similes, to augment their work with vivid images

3 Creative principles such as Show Don't Tell and surface versus depth

4 Dramatic techniques such as set-up and pay-off, or recasting traits and values.

Now we'll focus on bringing it all together line by line on the page. In the next chapter, on creative style, we'll begin by exploring the secrets of one of the most popular non-fiction genres: travel writing.

Ideas and inspirations

▶ Creative non-fiction authors exploit all the perspectives and techniques of dramatic writing.

▶ The non-fiction form can offer greater dramatic power to an author than even a novel, as we saw in *The Perfect Storm*.

▶ Non-fiction frees authors to use sophisticated techniques, such as Sobel's circular or helix-shaped narrative structure (rarely seen in storytelling, but see Tarantino's movie *Jackie Brown*).

▶ The standard three-act structure can anchor even complex narrative designs, in non-fiction as in fiction.

10 Writing style

In this chapter you will learn:

▶ Insider techniques of bestselling travel writers that inject that elusive page-turning quality into their work.

▶ About augmenting your natural style and writing persona by developing stylistic skills.

▶ Professional sentence designs, tried and tested to reduce clutter and inject pace into any kind of writing.

▶ Three handy techniques for sharpening up any piece of writing line by line.

→ ## Style in focus: Travel writing

The style on the page is paramount in travel writing, where the name of the game is turning that notebook of scribbled first impressions into sparkling prose.

Travel is something most of us are good at – who doesn't feel more alive, with no imperative on our time but to experience and enjoy? – but transforming subjective perspectives into insights anyone can share calls for a finely gauged writing style.

One technique exploited by market leaders is to match a carefully chosen tone of voice with a narrative persona that can act as a foil to their material. For Bill Bryson, the everyman persona of footsore tourist, perpetually in search of coffee and a sit-down, combines with a colloquial narrative style to create a breezily page-turning effect in bestsellers like *Neither Here nor There* and *Notes from a Small Island*.

Paul Theroux's narrative persona is in part generated by his material. Through a career established four decades ago with bestsellers like *The Great Indian Railway Bazaar*, Theroux's travels offer a rich mix of historical and cultural appreciation. The transcontinental railway lines of his journeys – amusingly supplanted by a kayak for his book on the Pacific islands, where canoes were until recently the only transport – are necessarily freighted with history, and take Theroux to the world's great (if often lesser-known) cultural centres.

A persona capable of mixing keen-eyed cultural analysis with enthusiastic historical and aesthetic appreciation has therefore proved the perfect mix for Theroux's books about crossing Africa, the Indian subcontinent, and even the tiny far-flung isles of the Pacific. Building a 'first person' in the text who is specifically designed to make the most of the material at hand is a writerly choice that opens up creative options in travel pieces.

Exercise 49

NARRATIVE PERSONA IN TRAVEL WRITING

Consider these three travel writing projects:

1. A pub tour of rural Ireland

2. An anthropological journey into the heart of Amazonia, living with local tribes and imbibing their religious psychedelics

3. A hard-trail hike through the Kathmandu valley

Which of the following travel personas do you think would bring most value to each project?

a. A gap-year student

b. A man having a mid-life crisis

c. A woman taking a vacation before trying to get pregnant

The important thing here is not whether your answers are the same as mine, but that you think about the processes you go through as you make your decision; the questions you ask of the material, and the strategic assessments you make. Match the numbers to the letters, and jot a couple of notes about how you came to each of your decisions if you can:

1. A pub tour of rural Ireland

2. An anthropological journey into the heart of Amazonia

3. A hard-trail hike through the Kathmandu valley

_____

_____

_____

_____

_____

_____

_____

_____

_____

_____

_____

_____

_____

_____

_____

_____

_____

_____

My answer to this question would run something like this: the guy having the mid-life crisis would have a whale of a time in Ireland for the first few days but would not prosper on a diet of Guinness and whisky; but the woman seeking to reconnect with herself before an important life step might find the bonhomie of Irish country pubs, and the beauty of the Emerald Isle landscape, just the tonic.

The gap-year student might enjoy the adventure of living with the tribe, though any growing up he has to do will be at the locals' expense; and certainly psychedelics should not be explored by those whose brains are still physically developing. However, the mid-life crisis man might find a rainforest reality check entirely beneficial, and the chance to look deep within, courtesy of a few Amazonian seeds and vines, mightn't be overdue. I think the gap-year student would best expend his energies, not on hoisting pints of porter, but finding himself through slog and self-sufficiency in the wild country around Kathmandu.

Choosing the right project is especially tough for travel writers, who need to balance personal desire and call-to-adventure emotions with making decisions about material that can make the most of their own particular insights and perspectives. It's possible to tweak your natural persona by augmenting it with research, whether academic or practical, but it's important to be thorough. If you want to write a surf odyssey, meaning to learn to surf when you reach the warm places of your trip, don't! – learn to surf locally, even if it means long car trips, and get competent before you set out. If you don't, you won't fit in locally and the worldwide fraternity of surfers – which can open a lot of doors in far-flung places – won't be open to you.

The same goes for learning to swim, bike, hike or climb, or appreciate wine or architecture or even local art and custom. Make your research meaningful, even if it means learning new skills six months or more before you approach the project: time spent in research, particularly of the hands-on practical variety, is never time wasted for a creative mind.

→ Style: Putting experience on the page

All creative authors, from memoirists to poets to travel writers, need to master style. The proof of your pudding as a writer – the cut of your jib, not to mention the straightness of your bat – needs to be in the words on the page. Readers won't know how worth reading you are if it's not there in black and white.

For many, mastering style is the first great breakthrough in their writing – the moment when what's on their page first begins to match up, in terms of reading experience, with the work of writers they admire. It can take a while, because your developing skills continue to fall short of standards set by your reading, but it's important to remember that mastering style is a process, but one of inexorable progress. As you add to your skills, your competence grows: it's as simple and rewarding as that.

So in this chapter we'll explore tools and techniques authors use in their writing style across genres:

▶ to create mood, using set-up passages to build atmosphere and pace simultaneously

▶ to heighten immediacy, with powerful constructions and quick-step clauses

▶ to slow the pace, foregrounding nuance and heightening emotional impact

▶ to maximize options in all stylistic choice making.

Let's look at specific techniques creative authors use line by line on the page to maximize the potential of their chosen material.

→ Pace and power, line by line: Using 'big-truck' sentences

The problem all creative writers face when they sit down to write is that they have a lot to say – many perspectives and insights and observations to transmit, but only the tight little structures of well-balanced sentences to convey it all on the page.

Much of the pleasure and art of writing is finding those succinct sentences, but writing is a business of set-up and pay-off. Sometimes the set-up has more complexity than even a succession of short sentences can convey, and sometimes the pay-off does, too. But as any comedian will tell you, the key to structuring set-up and pay-off is timing; so in these all too frequent situations, where the page needs zip but the material needs space, creative writers turn to their toolbox to solve the problem.

A popular writerly technique many use is the **big-truck sentence**. It's a special sentence design that allows writers to pack a lot of information into a few sequenced clauses. It's used most often in non-fiction, where establishing the full picture is a priority, and where necessary and often complex information must be delivered to the reader.

The big-truck sentence is structured to solve a very specific problem: one main clause that needs to carry several necessary sub-clauses. If you're not sure what a clause is, then the first part of this sentence up to the first comma is the main clause; the last piece of information you just read is a sub-clause – as is this and what precedes it. The big-truck sentence design allows a writer to pack information tightly before delivering the pay-off.

Back in the day, when trains were the predominant form of transport, this writerly construction was known as a locomotive sentence. Think of a big diesel engine pulling a line of freight cars, or a big-truck ballooning dust as it hauls hay-stacked flatbeds through the Texas badlands.

Here's the kind of information-dense set-up paragraph a big-truck sentence is designed to solve:

> *Ancient Hawaiian surfers were not like modern wave-riders, with their lightweight fibreglass boards. Old-style surfboards were big – up to 18 feet in length – and heavy, needing to be made from hardwood. Enthusiasts who've built replicas find them tiring to paddle and manoeuvre because of this extra weight. But surfing was both a royal and a national sport in the days of the Hawaiian kings, so old-style wooden surfboards are challenging but effective to ride – some modern-day enthusiasts even prefer them when surf conditions are optimal.*

There's nothing here that's too burdensome to read, and to an enthusiast it delivers all the information you'd want to know – if you'd seen someone riding an old-style hardwood board, for example, and googled 'wooden surfboards' when you got home. The paragraph would make a reasonable caption to a blog photo of an old Hawaiian surfing scene, perhaps.

But, although it's a coherent and reasonably effective piece of writing, it's slow to read. There's little sense of pace. If this paragraph wasn't a blog caption, but appeared in a non-fiction book about surfing, and occurred in the middle of a couple of pages of similar paragraphs, then this would perhaps seem like a slow couple of pages to a reader, for all the information delivered. It's a slow read.

This is exactly the kind of problem the big-truck technique was designed to solve. The paragraph on surfing above, with its four long and complicated sentences, can be rewritten as a single, comprehensive big-truck sentence:

> *Old-style Hawaiian surfboards were big and heavy, up to three times the size of today's fibreglass decks; but though their solid hardwood makes them challenging to ride, some modern-day purists still ride old-style when the surf's up.*

It's not a sparkling transformation, but all the information is delivered in around half the space: a sense of pace, and of forward movement, is built into the big-truck version.

Slimming a paragraph of written-up notes down into a sleeker big-truck construction means eliminating repetition, fine-tuning and honing the material, making bolder decisions with word choices – for example, I used the technical term 'deck' for surfboard in the big-truck sentence above. I chose this, rather than repeat the original noun, even in its slimmed-down version of 'board', because the insider term I used lets a reader decode the lingo for him- or herself and feel a little more involved in the world being described. Similarly, the colloquial 'surf's up' condenses the last clause of the first version, adding a visual element just as 'deck' did. In both cases, observing the rule of Show Don't Tell assists both in condensing the material and in creating the big-truck construction.

Exercise 50

CREATING BIG-TRUCK SENTENCES

Read the following travel-piece opening, and make notes on it where you think the material could be honed. It's a long paragraph, so expect to use three big-truck sentences, but if you can make it shorter without losing anything, then go for it:

→ It's a long way from the Chelsea-tractor school run for a young girl and her kid brother in northern China. Every school day the 11-year-old must walk hand in hand with her five-year-old sibling through the jungle from their mountainside farm, where their family has grown tea for generations, to the side of a terrifyingly precipitous river valley, and the zip wire across it that is their only transport. There the little girl must bundle her brother into a sack – he's too young to suppress automatic panic reactions at the gaping gulf below – then hook him on to the zip wire, cobbled together by her father, and climb into the sack herself. Then she leaps into space. For three heart-stopping minutes the pair travel at speeds approaching 60 miles an hour, the little girl braking with a forked piece of wood, until they land safely on the far side of the vast river valley. At the end of the school day, they must perform the feat again in reverse.

_____

Now write your three big-truck sentences:

_____

_____

_____

_____

_____

_____

_____

_____

_____

_____

_____

If you managed to get all that down into three shortish sentences then well done. Perhaps you came up with something like this:

For a northern Chinese little girl and her brother, the daily school run from the family tea farm means zip-lining – on cables Dad tinkered together – high above a precipitous mountain valley. Each morning, the five-year-old boy – too young to cope with the dizzying gulf below – must climb into a sack before his 11-year-old sister hooks him on to the wire, and climbs on herself. Then she pushes off into the void, hurtling high above the valley at 60 miles per hour or more, braking with nothing more than a forked timber; at the end of each school day she repeats the feat, in reverse.

In the above example, honing and rearranging the material adds a sense of pace that builds with the narration. The second sentence, for example, begins with the brother's youth, making the use of the sack the intriguing set-up to the sentence, before one reads why the sack is necessary – a pattern of set-up and pay-off in a single sentence, itself the pay-off to the paragraph. Stylistically, you'll notice the brevity of the final pay-off clause – a two-word rhythmic quickstep that slingshots the reader toward the next paragraph – itself made possible by careful use of multi-clause constructions.

Winnowing and sharpening first-draft material, and trying big-truck constructions with the results, makes it possible to apply and reapply the technique to material until your line-by-line pacing feels right.

→ Description: Associative choices versus oppositional choices

When you're working on sharpening your descriptive powers, it can be helpful to stop reaching for natural associations – yellow like a yellow thing, sweet like a sweet thing – and move your thinking to another sphere entirely; a world, even, quite different from that of the thing you're describing.

This is called 'oppositional' imagery – rather than deriving from an associative process, it generates power with the friction of opposites. Obviously, your 'opposites' need to come from a more thoughtful process, but building 'opposite sphere' imagery – rather than following the naturally associative writerly mental searches for original and striking imagery we all make when seeking to enliven descriptive writing – can make a workaday figurative device into a striking one.

When creating 'oppositional' imagery, creative writers think outside the box. Instead of looking for associations from within the same world as the subject of the image, in order to build a simile or metaphor – saying A is like B, or C is as D – the creative writer using oppositional imagery will go to another sphere entirely – for example using a homely image to describe a disturbing event.

It's perfectly natural, when you're trying to come up with original descriptive imagery, to make associative connections in your initial thinking. It's how we describe things, in everyday terms: the sky out to sea on a midwinter morning has all the iridescent blues of a mackerel's back, for example.

Sometimes an associative approach is effective; but when it isn't, thinking outside the box can free things up. In a piece about an autopsy, novelist and journalist Helen Garner wrote about a morgue technician scouring out a dead person's skull:

> *...using the same rounded, firm, deliberate movements of wrist and hand that my grandmother would use to rub out a small saucepan.*

It's an arresting, surprising, yet very satisfying image: which is good, because anything that fell short of achieving this effect would be gruesome, and probably need to be cut from the final draft. But with her unexpected image, which zeroes in not on the gore or existential elements – the obvious associative directions to follow – but on fine description of what's actually happening, the author achieves a deeper involvement from her readers with the world of the piece, and the dexterity and dedication she's witnessing. By taking an image from an 'opposite' world to a cold silent morgue – a grandmother's busy kitchen – Garner both surprises her reader and draws them in to her tale.

CREATING FRESH IMAGERY

Pick a descriptive passage you've particularly enjoyed from a book on your shelves, and see if you can identify the types of imagery it uses. Is much of the imagery associational, where like is being compared to like? Or is the author mixing it up a little, using oppositional imagery like the saucepan-scrubbing grandma above?

Pick out the key imagery below, and see if you can work associational imagery into an oppositional example, something from another sphere of life entirely. Or, if your chosen piece is taking risks to achieve powerful effects, see if you can reverse-engineer the processes used to create the complex image, right back to the original associative 'like for like' comparison if you can:

_____

_____

_____

_____

_____

_____

_____

_____

_____

_____

_____

_____

_____

_____

_____

_____

_____

_____

_____

_____

_____

_____

_____

Sometimes it's a real pleasure to work through the options with a piece or sequence of imagery, and sometimes it can seem like the kind of genius comparison that comes only with lightning-bolt inspiration. But training your mind to work with the options in image construction – the different seams of material that can be mined by using associative or oppositional thinking – is what makes your creativity a fertile place for striking and intriguing images to form, as if on their own. Just as smart people make their luck, smart writers make their 'inspiration' happen, with the development of skills and abilities you're achieving as you work through this book.

→ Keeping it fresh on the page: three tricks

Finding an arresting phrase, to pep up a passage exactly where it needs it most, is much of the creative writer's line-by-line legwork. Here are three tips worth trying, when you're reaching for that intriguing image or phrase:

1. REVERSE THE CLICHÉ

Take a tired phrase and turn it around. For example, rather than saying 'It couldn't happen to a nicer guy' with sour irony when someone unpleasant receives good fortune, try 'It could happen to a nicer guy'. Eliminating the tired irony of the cliché gives a fresh spin to the familiar.

2. PUSH THE METRIC

This technique is especially useful in descriptive writing that makes multiple comparisons. For example:

He was a big man, around six feet five and the same across.

Not a bad sentence, if a little familiar in its closing pay-off. Yet look what Raymond Chandler did with it, in the opening lines of *Farewell, My Lovely:*

> *He was a big man but not more than six feet five inches tall and not wider than a beer truck.*

By pushing the 'metric' of the first comparison – the dimensions of this man – the unexpected, amusing closing phrase tells us all we need to know about this guy, Moose Malloy, and what it would be like to tangle with him.

3. EXPLOIT REPETITION

Good writers prune repetition, so when used deliberately it can have powerful effect. In the opening of his non-fiction bestseller *The Tipping Point*, Malcolm Gladwell exploits repetition of the word 'idea' to make a complex proposition seem approachable:

> *The Tipping Point is the biography of an idea, and the idea is very simple.*

It's anything but, and the long sentence that follows deploys a big-truck construction to explain that this book will examine the phenomenon of things becoming massively popular, from slang phrases to fashion trends to phenomena like Harry Potter and *Fifty Shades of Grey*. The final line of the paragraph returns to simplicity, after the necessary complexity of the set-up, for the pay-off, the book's first big assertion:

> *Ideas and products and messages and behaviors spread just like viruses do.*

Repetition of the foregrounded word 'idea' is deployed here to link back to the idea of the first line – carrying the associative implication that the author's project is at heart approachable as well as illuminating.

FRESHENING UP SENTENCES

Let's try some of these creative approaches in action.

1. Reversing the cliché

Write down all the everyday clichés you hear that drive you nuts on a daily basis. Can you re-spin any (remember the example: 'It couldn't happen to a nicer guy' / 'It could happen to a nicer guy'). Taking irony out of this example freshens and re-spins it: Can you do this with your pet peeve phrases?

_____

_____

_____

_____

_____

_____

_____

_____

_____

_____

_____

_____

_____

2. Push the metric

Describe yourself at age 15. Take some time to dig out old photos and reminisce if it helps. Concentrate on one aspect in particular, like how that perennial concern of young teens – physical appearance – projected, perhaps, nerdiness rather than the suavity you were aiming for. Try to boil a portrait down to a few sentences, by focusing on one key aspect.

Now see if you can exploit that focus on one key aspect to extend the 'metric' – the way you're 'measuring' – throughout your portrait.

_____

_____

_____

_____

_____

_____

_____

_____

_____

_____

Were you able to find a 'metric' and extend it? I came up with this:

> *I was tall but barely a hundred pounds, most of them accounted for by elbows.*

I've used a colloquialism here – we describe someone awkward as being 'all elbows' – to anchor this 'pushing the metric'. The image of a gawky, awkward teenager emerges, after the reader has been given a small, amusing riddle to solve. That reader engagement we all strive for can often be elicited in this way.

3. Exploit repetition

Try to think of a few snatches of favourite writing that exploit repetition. Spend some time with your bookshelves if you can't think of any offhand. Poems might spring to mind first, but literary and even comic novels exploit the technique often, particularly in scene-setting and descriptive passages.

If you're stuck for examples, try these opening lines from Charles Dickens's *Our Mutual Friend*:

In these times of ours, though concerning the exact year there is no need to be precise, a boat of dirty and disreputable appearance, with two figures in it, floated on the Thames, between Southwark bridge which is of iron, and London Bridge which is of stone, as an autumn evening was closing in.

The figures in this boat were those of a strong man with ragged grizzled hair and a sun-browned face, and a dark girl of nineteen or twenty, sufficiently like him to be recognizable as his daughter. The girl rowed, pulling a pair of sculls very easily; the man, with the rudder-lines slack in his hands, and his hands loose in his waistband, kept an eager look out. He had no net, hook, or line, and he could not be a fisherman; his boat had no cushion for a sitter, no paint, no inscription, no appliance beyond a rusty boathook and a coil of rope, and he could not be a waterman; his boat was too crazy and too small to take in cargo for delivery, and he could not be a lighterman or river-carrier; there was no clue to what he looked for, but he looked for something, with a most intent and searching gaze. The tide, which had turned an hour before, was running down, and his eyes watched every little race and eddy in its broad sweep, as the boat made slight head-way against it, or drove stern foremost before it, according as he directed his daughter by a movement of his head. She watched his face as earnestly as he watched the river. But in the intensity of her look there was a touch of dread or horror.

Can you identify where and how repetition is exploited? What's the effect achieved? What other techniques – alliteration and other sonorous word choices, in the above example – are also deployed, to maximize the effect?

_____

_____

_____

_____

_____

_____

_____

_____

_____

→ Writing dialogue

All creative writers may need to write dialogue: dramatists do little else, of course, but life writers and travel authors, even poets (think of the exquisitely timed 'my head is bad tonight' sequence in Eliot's *The Waste Land,* for example).

The rules of Show Don't Tell and Less Is More are paramount in dialogue. People generally try to show what they mean – often in confusing or convoluted ways – rather than saying what they mean outright. Even people who boast that they say what they mean and mean what they say are, of course, saying something else entirely.

The key to dialogue is to stop it sounding like dialogue. It's as simple as that. If you find yourself falling into a back-and-forth rhythm – he said, she said, he mused, she interjected – get out of there fast.

Instead, exploit the fractured nature of most everyday conversations: their circularities, intonations, repetitions and tendency to wander off at tangents. Tune your ear to conversations going on around you – on the commute, at the supermarket, buying lunch – and pick up on the devices people use to keep their conversation fresh, and stop it becoming linear and predictable. It's the latter that dogs most authors when they try to write dialogue, so let's try an exercise to explore some techniques of good dialogue in detail.

Exercise 53

FRESHENING DIALOGUE

Make notes on the following exchange of dialogue. Circle words or phrases where you feel the tightness of the exchange beginning to slip:

→ 'It was nothing,' she said, relieved. 'Really, that's all that's been bothering you?'

→ 'Well,' he said, 'most people wouldn't call it nothing.'

→ She looked at him. 'Really. Come here.'

→ He stayed where he was.

→ 'It was nothing,' she said, less breezily now, 'a stupid drunk thing. A meaningless Christmas fling. You weren't around. I was just trying to keep my chin up, going to the party in the first place.'

→ He didn't respond. She persisted.

→ 'Christmas and you away: you know the pressure to drink, season to be jolly and all that. A stupid drunk thing, a long time ago. Seriously, five years…'

→ 'He was my best friend,' he cut in. 'How am I supposed to be with him now? Knowing that you…'

→ 'For heaven's sake,' she interjected. 'What matters is the here and now, not some silly drunken night that happened five years ago. What we've built together, what we've got. Seriously, we're the lucky ones.'

→ He looked at her, wanting to believe. She looked back, then put a hand on her hip.

→ 'So you want to get lucky?' she said.

It's a quick-fire scene and works with some difficult emotions briskly. But there's a lot of back-and-forth in it, and it may well be that establishing this back-and-forth rhythm disrupts the larger rhythm of the passage containing this scene – or just perhaps that a shorter dialogue scene would have more power.

You've probably made a few notes. The exchange spends a good few utterances establishing the basic facts and emotions: these can be pruned down. Most of the dialogue attribution (the 'he said' and 'she said' phrases) can be cut: they're telling the reader how to interpret, not showing, what's going on – the utterances alone should be capable of carrying the sense. And some of the back-and-forth nature of the power balance in the scene could be tightened up dramatically: the scene as it stands covers all the emotions, but it may be possible to distil the back-and-forth of this scene to its dramatic core. Is it possible to start the scene later into the action than it currently begins? Or end it earlier?

Try to work on these aspects as you attempt your own rewrite of the scene here:

_____

_____

_____

_____

_____

_____

_____

_____

_____

_____

_____

_____

_____

Focusing on pace and impact can open up ways to rewrite a scene. In this example, some repetition regarding each character's relative positions in the scene can certainly be cut. The scene can also start 'later' – it spends a little while in the above draft establishing that he's offended and she's trying to be pragmatic. The words used to attribute dialogue – 'he cut in', 'she interjected' – can be simplified because where one utterance cuts across another is plain. Here's my revised version:

> She said, 'I don't appreciate that tone.'
>
> 'What else do you want to call it?' His voice was angry now.
>
> 'What matters is here and now,' she said, 'not five years ago.'
>
> 'He was my buddy,' he said. 'And all this time I thought...
>
> 'You thought what? You were a lucky son of a gun? Well, you are. We are. What we do with that predicament is our choice,' she said, and cocked a hip and an eyebrow both at once.

Where to next?

I hope you've found this book a helpful grounding in some of the basic tools and techniques creative writers use to bring their work to life on the page, and that my exercises have stimulated your creative thinking. Learning to write creatively is a steep uphill climb for all of us, so remember that there are many others out there who share your energy and passion – as well as the everyday frustrations of all budding writers. Local writers' groups and online forums alike are a great way to share tips and techniques, gallows humour and mutual support, so get out there with your writing – you'll find that many others enjoy the satisfaction and pleasure of developing creative skills. Evening-class courses run by colleges and universities are another excellent way to learn and develop amongst peers.

Finding creative fulfilment is a long road, best taken step by step with good humour and company.

Ideas and inspirations

▶ Creative authors use stylistic tricks and techniques to create that elusive page-turning quality in their work.

▶ Genres like travel writing can powerfully exploit a narrative 'persona', as a foil to the line-by-line style dictated by the material.

▶ Pace and power can be locked down line by line using the big-truck sentence technique.

▶ Other writerly tricks such as 'pushing the metric', or exploiting patterns in word choices, are easily practised tools that liberate and enhance creativity.

Afterword: The five creative choices

If you've made it this far, then well done! That was a lot of ground covered, and I hope your appetite is whetted for more self-development in your journey as an author.

But I know from my own experience that one of the toughest obstacles all budding writers face comes from within. It's because you've read well that you want to be a writer; but, now that you're writing, your good reading is telling you that no matter what progress you make, it's impossible ever to measure up to the authors you admire.

It's completely natural to feel this way, and everyone does. What isn't natural is to let it get you down. No one knows how good they're going to be until, with practice and self-development, they suddenly are.

And that's the natural outcome of the journey you're on right now: you will surprise yourself, soon. And keep on surprising yourself with how accomplished your writing is starting to look, until accomplishment flows from your fingertips each time you sit down to write.

So let's revisit, as a checklist, some of the ideas and perspectives we've worked with in this book.

A creative author begins at the beginning. When they take on a project, they lay out their narrative options like tools on a workbench. They're not just looking for a good way 'in' to a piece, because they know that will come naturally – from making the best choices about what tools and colours from their creative palette to use.

CHOICE 1: STRUCTURE

Is there a beginning, a middle and an end to this project's central idea? If not there are two options: develop the idea, or have sufficient genius to deploy your material in opposition to a reader's expectations about structure. The first of these options is most likely to yield results.

Creating beginnings, middles, and endings from a glimmer of an idea is nothing to be feared. It's how thinking people have approached problems since time immemorial. A construction contractor will assess a job, deliver a plan, get materials and manpower in place, then execute the project: a three-phase approach. Ancient Greek philosophers similarly used a classic three-phase approach to all the thorniest questions: thesis – hypothesis – synthesis.

So your job when teasing an idea out into a fully-fledged creation is to find its natural three-part structure of beginning, middle, and end – and once more we start at the beginning.

CHOICE 2: NARRATOR

Who is the teller of your tale? Even with autobiography or memoir, the answer is never 'the person writing it'. The job of a creative author is to maximize their options in constructing the persona on the page. This is a fine time for blue-sky thinking: who would you most want to hear this idea from, if you were to get really fired-up about it? Who's your ideal narrator for this piece?

Narrowing down whom you really want to hear about your chosen project from puts a human side to your idea. Your brain takes over at this point, being a finely-engineered machine for gauging human qualities: at the top of the food chain, the predator's only fear is others like him. So ideas and colour start to flow at this point, putting 'flesh on the bones' of your idea, and giving you the inklings of the best way to make Choice Number 1 above.

CHOICE 3: SHOW DON'T TELL

As I hope you now feel confident, the rule of 'show don't tell' is your creative partner when you write. It's what opens up scenes and created scenarios, giving a reader the keys to your world and a guiding hand once they're in there with you.

Show don't tell will help you set the scene of your creative piece effectively, exploiting the tension between location and milieu to bring your words to life on the page.

CHOICE 4: MAKING CHARACTERS COME ALIVE

Even if the only character in your creative piece is a soda-can tumbling toward a rain-swollen storm drain, it will be brought to vivid and thought-provoking life by mining the narrative gold which lies between initial *characterization* and developing *deep character*. The soda-can in this hypothetical poem or vignette looks like any other discarded can – but in literature focus delivers meaning. This tin can is not what it initially appears, and will be used to explore an interesting perspective or truth.

CHOICE 5: CHARACTER PROGRESSION, ARCS AND VALUES, RESONANCE AND MEANING

This is where creativity comes together and deep meaning emerges. Using real human experience to build the deep foundation of your creative piece, in building character-arcs and engineering value-progressions, is how you give your project a sturdy and serviceable pair of wings, and a fair wind. Far from limiting creativity by 'applying formulas', making use of the tried-and-tested arc and value progressions which authors have used since the dawn of storytelling unleashes the full creative energy and deep meaning of your work.

So it boils down to five big choices, and the rest is up to you. Very best of luck, and look out for more Creative Writing Workbooks coming soon!

Glossary of terms

Act, Dramatic (n.) – A coherent sequence of dramatic scenes or short movements (in a novel, memoir, travel book, poem, screenplay, etc.) which build typically to a mid-act climax and an act climax.

Act Climax – The culmination of a dramatic Act. It both pays-off what has come before and slingshots the creative piece forward into its next movement.

Antagonist – The protagonist's true adversary in a story. This is often not the perpetrator of the crime or event which triggers the story.

Arc, Character (n. & v.) – The human change a character or narrator/protagonist undergoes through the course of a creative piece.

Characterization – How a character is presented when they first appear in a creative piece.

Character, deep – How a character is developed by the events of a creative piece.

Core Value – The idea at the heart of a creative work, in the same kind of way that a song or movie has a 'message'.

Core Value Progression – A coherent development of core-value idea(s) to tell a human truth.

Drama – The rhetorical animation of ideas.

Location – The geographical setting of a creative piece.

Milieu – The set of particular circumstances that make this location a birthing-ground for story.

Plot – Progression of a core value (e.g. the value of LOYALTY to self: in Orwell's *Nineteen Eighty-Four* the progression is SPLIT ALLEGIANCE LOYALTY BETRAYAL SELF-BETRAYAL).

Protagonist – The heroine or hero (sometimes the narrator) who undergoes most meaningful human change over the course of a creative piece.

Villain – Sometimes the villain is the antagonist, sometimes (as in *The Silence of the Lambs*, or Jane Austen novels) the villain is just the perpetrator.

Bibliography

Browning, R., *Selected Poems* (London: Penguin, 2000)

Dickens, C., *Our Mutual Friend* (Oxford: Oxford University Press, 2008)

Dickinson, E., *Emily Dickinson*, Everyman Poetry (London: Phoenix, 1997)

Eliot, T. S., *Selected Poems of T. S. Eliot* (London: Faber & Faber, 2002)

Frost, R., *Robert Frost's Poems* (New York: St. Martin's Press, 2002)

Golding, W., *Lord of the Flies* (London: Faber & Faber, 1997)

Hardy, T., *Selected Poems* (London: Penguin, 1993)

Joyce, J., *Poems and Shorter Writings* (London: Faber & Faber, 2001)

Niven, D., *The Moon's a Balloon* (London: Penguin, 1994)

Orwell, G., *Nineteen-Eighty-Four* (London: Penguin, 2013)

Owen, W., *The War Poems of Wilfred Owen* (London: Chatto & Windus, 1994)

Raine, C., *Collected Poems, 1978–1998* (London: Picador, 2000)

Saunders, G., 'The End of FIRPO in the World', in *Pastoralia* (New York: Penguin, 2000)

Sobel, D., *Longitude: The True Story of a Lone Genius Who Solved the Greatest Scientific Problem of His Time*, 10th anniversary edn (London: Harper Perennial, 2005)

Trethewy, N., 'Incident', in *Native Guard* (New York: Houghton Mifflin Harcourt, 2007)

Index